THE
PHILOSOPHY
OF CHABAD

ב"ה

The Philosophy of Chabad

Rabbi Schneur Zalman of Liadi
Vol. 2

by
NISSAN MINDEL

CHABAD RESEARCH CENTER
KEHOT PUBLICATION SOCIETY
770 Eastern Parkway / Brooklyn, NY 11213

The Philosophy of Chabad
Rabbi Schneur Zalman of Liadi Vol. 2

Copyright © 1973-1985
First Edition—Three Printings

Revised Edition © 2007
by
KEHOT PUBLICATION SOCIETY
770 Eastern Parkway • Brooklyn, New York 11213
(718) 774-4000 • FAX (718) 774-2718

Order Department:
291 Kingston Avenue • Brooklyn, New York 11213
(718) 778-0226 • FAX (718) 778-4148
www.kehotonline.com

Library of Congress Cataloging-in-Publication Data
Mindel, Nissan.
The philosophy of Chabad.
Includes bibliographical references and index.
1. Habad. 2. Shneur Zalman, of Lyady, 1745-1813. 3. Judaism Doctrines. I. Shneur
Zalman, of Lyady, 1745-1813. Likute amarim.
English. Selections. 1985.
II. Title.

BM98.M48 1985   296.3'092'4   85-18230

ISBN: 978-0-8266-0417-0

Manufactured in the United States of America

CONTENTS

I. THE HUMAN PERSONALITY

II. THE COSMIC ENTITY

III. ENDS AND MEANS

IV. THE FULFILLMENT

SUPPLEMENT

PREFACE

The present volume is an attempt at presenting an outline of Rabbi Schneur Zalman's thought, namely, the Chabad philosophical system which he created. It complements the biographical volume on the founder of the Chabad movement, penned by this writer and published previously.[1]

The basis for this outline is, primarily, Rabbi Schneur Zalman's *Likkutei Amarim* (*Tanya*), the celebrated Chabad classic, which, as we had occasion to note elsewhere, is regarded as the "Written Law" (*Torah shebiktav*) of Chabad. Occasionally, other works of Rabbi Schneur Zalman were used as sources of reference. However, the writer hopes to produce a further volume on R. Schneur Zalman's philosophy, based mainly on the latter's two other basic works, *Torah Or* and *Likkutei Torah*, in order to present a more comprehensive account of R. Schneur Zalman's thought.

To make up for the conciseness and "capsule form" of the present outline, and since it contains very little in the way of direct quotation from R. Schneur Zalman's works, this volume has been provided with a Supplement of selected readings from the *Tanya* (Part I), which have a direct bearing on the main topics of this volume. In this way, the serious reader and student will be able not only to broaden his knowledge of the subjects treated herein, but will also have an opportunity of acquainting himself with the style and method of the author's own exposition.

Few luminaries in Jewish history, particularly in modern times, have made such a lasting contribution to the spiritual heritage of our people as R. Schneur Zalman, founder of Chabad. His works, embracing the whole spectrum of Jewish thought—

Halachah, Kabbalah, Jewish philosophy, and ethics—place him among the most creative spiritual giants in many a century. The fact that his Chabad system has become a way of life for a large segment of world Jewry, and is constantly winning new adherents among the seekers of Truth, especially within the ranks of the new generation, is clear testimony of the viability and relevance of the Chabad religious philosophy in the present day and age, as it was some two centuries ago at the time of its inception.

The present volume can serve only as a general introduction to the philosophy of Chabad. For a fuller and deeper knowledge of it, the reader and student must turn to R. Schneur Zalman's original works, as well as to the "Oral Law" of Chabad, the vast Chabad literature which has accumulated over the past seven generations of Chabad leaders, including the present head of Chabad, Rabbi Menachem Schneerson, the Lubavitcher Rebbe שליט״א.

The publication date of this volume has been set for the 18th ("Chai") Elul, the birthday of R. Schneur Zalman, as also of R. Yisrael Baal Shem Tov, the father of General Chasidut, whose teachings served R. Schneur Zalman as the wellspring of his Chabad philosophy and way of life.

In conclusion, a word of thanks to my esteemed colleagues at the Chabad Research Center for perusal of the manuscript and helpful suggestions; to my wife Nettie, for editorial assistance and proofreading, and to my daughter Frida Schapiro, for the Index.

NISSAN MINDEL

18th of Elul, 5733
Long Beach, N. Y.

---

1. Nissan Mindel, *Rabbi Schneur Zalman of Liadi*, Vol. 1, Kehot Publication Society, Brooklyn, N.Y., 1969. Revised Edition, 2002.

INTRODUCTION

I

In the preceding volume, the biography of Rabbi Shneur Zalman,[1] an attempt was made to trace the origins of the Chasidic movement, founded by Rabbi Yisrael Baal Shem Tov, whose spiritual "grandson" the founder of the Chabad branch of General Chasidut considered himself.[2] Having followed the life and work of Rabbi Schneur Zalman, his childhood and formative years, his "conversion" to Chasidut, and his dedication to all that it stood for, the reader will have gleaned some insights into his personality, aspirations, and the driving forces and circumstances which impelled him to assume the pastoral leadership of the many thousands of his followers, and, particularly, to create his Chabad system of Jewish religious philosophy.

In the present volume an attempt will be made to present a general outline, as concise as possible, of Rabbi Schneur Zalman's central thoughts and ideas underlying his Chabad system. This attempt is made not without trepidation, because of the depth of the subject and the inadequacy of the interpreter.

The task is a formidable one; not only because of the abstruseness of the ideas and doctrines with which one has to cope—since, basically, Chabad is rooted in Jewish mysticism, the Kabbalah, but also because of the intrinsic nature of the sources. Most of Rabbi Schneur Zalman's works were originally not writ-

---

1. Nissan Mindel, *Rabbi Schneur Zalman of Liadi*, Vol. 1 (Kehot), 1969. Revised Edition, 2002.
2. Ibid., pp. 27, 102.

1

ten in a systematic manner for students of philosophy. A notable exception is the *Tanya*, or *Likkutei Amarim*, in its first three parts, each a separate treatise, in which a unified presentation is given. His other major works, the *Torah Or* and *Likkutei Torah*, are actually a collection of independent essays arranged according to the Hebrew calendar of Sabbatical readings from the Pentateuch and other Biblical references pertaining to the festivals. Long before these essays were committed to writing, they were preached orally by way of sermons and discourses. The same is true of the *Tanya*, which, in parts, also consists of epistles and pastoral letters sent to the faithful, or even to individuals, at different times and on different occasions, over a period of some forty years. Moreover, with the exception of the first three sections of the *Tanya*, Rabbi Schneur Zalman's Chabad works were published posthumously, so that they were not edited by the author himself.

The difficulties of the task are further compounded by the general problem of rendering into English—categories and concepts originally expounded in Hebrew and Yiddish, in a style and in terms peculiar to the author. Fortunately, the problem of semantics had been largely dealt with when the *Tanya* was first translated.[3]

As far as this writer knows, no attempt has been made before to present a comprehensive interpretation of Chabad in any language, least of all in English.[4] If the present volume is, therefore, something in the nature of a pioneer effort in a virgin field, the writer can only hope that this consideration will perhaps mitigate the shortcomings of his contribution.

---

3. *Likkutei Amarim* [*Tanya*] (Kehot), Part One, tr. Nissan Mindel, 1st ed. 1962, 2nd ed. 1965, 3rd ed. (revised), 1969; Part Two, tr. Nissen Mangel, 1965; Part Three, tr. Zalman I. Posner, 1st ed. 1965, 2nd ed. 1968; Part Four, tr. Jacob I. Schochet, 1968; Part Five, tr. Zalman I. Posner, 1968. Subsequently, all five parts have been published in one Hebrew-English volume and has seen numerous editions.
4. Works (in Hebrew) on the teachings of Chabad include the following: H. I. Bunin, *Mishne Chabad*, Warsaw 1936. M. Teitelbaum, *Harav miLadi umifleget chabad*, 2 vols. Warsaw 1910-13. Hilel Zeitlin, *Arainfir in chasidus un der veg fun chabad* (Yiddish), N.Y. 1957.

II

RABBI SCHNEUR ZALMAN'S philosophical system is basically a synthesis between the Kabbalah and the Halachah; between the mystical and rational currents of Jewish thought, which he blended rather remarkably well into one cohesive religious philosophy, generally known as Chabad.

An interpreter trying to establish a frame of reference for the interpretation of this system to the contemporary student of Judaism and Jewish religious philosophy, could have various options open to him.

It is possible, for instance, to attempt an evaluation of Rabbi Schneur Zalman's thought from the vantage point of any one or several particular philosophical approaches, such as rationalist Neoplatonic, empirical, pantheistic, existential, and so on. Undoubtedly it is possible to find in Chabad points of contact with many ideas and doctrines expressed in various schools of thought. However, at best, this would offer only a partial acquaintance with Rabbi Schneur Zalman's total outlook; at worst, the results might be tortuous or distorted.

Another approach might be to trace Rabbi Schneur Zalman's central ideas to their sources, since he himself never laid claim to originality in his teachings. Actually, this disclaimer on the author's part was largely prompted by a deep sense of modesty. His dependence on "scribes and books," which he mentions in his Foreword to the *Tanya*, is, of course, often in evidence by his frequent citation of sources. Nonetheless, many of his thoughts, ideas, and concepts are original, or have been so modified and transformed under his treatment as to give them the imprint of originality. It would be no easy task to embark upon a detailed analysis, and, more importantly, in this writer's opinion, the gain would not equal the effort.

At any rate, this writer has set himself the task of presenting a comprehensive review of Rabbi Schneur Zalman's thought as a whole. Consequently, the primary purpose of this study must be expository rather than analytical. However, in following this method there will be ample opportunity also to trace some of the basic ideas of Chabad to their original sources, and to relate them

3

to other trends in medieval Jewish philosophy, and to some extent to general philosophy, yet mindful of not deviating too much from the main purpose of the task at hand.

It should also be added that the present volume is in the main limited to the teachings and doctrines of the *Tanya*, which is only one of the classical sources of Chabad. It does not encompass all the teachings of Chabad, while those dealt with are by no means discussed with the depths with which they are expounded in the author's other, and more voluminous, works, the *Torah Or* and *Likkutei Torah*, as well as many others, both published and unpublished. It is projected that this volume will be followed by a further volume which will hopefully widen the horizons of Chabad to the interested student and reader.

III

IT HAS ALREADY BEEN NOTED[5] that the *Tanya* was written, as the author indicates in his Foreword, for the "seekers" and "perplexed." The same can be said of Rabbi Schneur Zalman's other philosophical writings.

One is tempted to draw a parallel between this author and his book and Maimonides and his *Guide*. Indeed, both men present some striking points in common. Each of them first established his reputation as a Talmudist and Codifier before entering the field of philosophy; both had written Codes of Jewish Law, which are still authoritative and popular. Each of them created a new and lasting school of thought in Jewish philosophy; and the one, like the other, set out to write a work which aimed at helping those who needed guidance in their religious beliefs. Yet both of them evoked sharp opposition from the orthodox faction; both were misunderstood, accused of heresy, and their philosophical treatises were banned and consigned to the flames.

However, this is as far as the parallel goes. The *Guide* and the *Tanya* represent two widely divergent systems, in essence as well as in form. The two authors were separated by some six centuries in time, and far apart also geographically and in respect of the whole cultural milieu in which they flourished. Maimonides is

---

5. Introduction to *Likkutei Amarim* [*Tanya*], Part One, op. cit., p. xvii ff.

the rational Jewish philosopher *par excellence*; Rabbi Schneur Zalman is basically a mystic. The "perplexed" for whom they wrote were two entirely different types of people. Maimonides wrote for the man whose perplexity derived from the fact that he desired to retain his traditional beliefs, but was puzzled by the apparent contradiction between tradition and philosophy, yet loath to give up either.[6] The object of the *Guide* therefore was to effect a reconciliation between the two.

No such problem confronted Rabbi Schneur Zalman. Philosophy and science hardly had a place among the masses of Eastern European Jewry at that time. The *Haskalah* movement had not yet made any serious inroads upon the minds of the masses. Rabbi Schneur Zalman addressed himself to those "who are in pursuit of righteousness and seek the Lord...whose intelligence and mind are confused and they wander about in darkness in the service of G-d, unable to perceive the beneficial light that is concealed in books."[7] In other words, he writes for those whose beliefs have not been troubled by doubts, but who merely seek the right path to G-d.

We will therefore not find in the *Tanya* or in any of Rabbi Schneur Zalman's other works the type of scholastic philosophy with which the *Guide* is replete, nor any polemics, nor even an attempt to treat systematically many of the philosophical problems which engaged Maimonides' attention. Such basic beliefs as the Existence of G-d, *creatio ex nihilo*, Revelation, and others, are taken for granted by the author. Others, such as the Divine attributes, Providence, Unity, Messianism, etc., are treated as integral parts of his ethical system, and illuminated by the light of the Kabbalah.

The main purpose of the *Tanya* is to serve as a practical manual, as it were, charting a new course in Divine service, with the various parts of the *Tanya* as "guidebooks" in this itinerary. Narrowing these down to their main objectives, we may describe them as follows: The first part is basically designed to develop the two fundamental principles of Divine worship, *ahava* and *yirah*,

---

6. *The Guide for the Perplexed*, tr. M. Freedlander, London 1942, Introduction, p. 2.
7. *Likkutei Amarim*, Part One, Compiler's Foreword, p. 9.

love and awe. The second part, in which the author expounds the Beshtian doctrine of Creation, aims at fostering true belief in G-d and in Divine Providence according to Chasidic concept. The third part is devoted to *teshuvah*, repentance, while the last two parts enlighten the worshipper on various aspects of the Divine commandments.

The *Tanya* is thus a unique and novel work on Jewish ethics: unique in its structure and novel in its approach. While the author is primarily concerned with the forces of good and evil in human nature and in the surrounding world, his objective (as already pointed out), is to pave a new way to the *summum bonum*. He is aware, of course, of the existence of Hebrew literature dealing with the same subject. If he is impelled to write a new book, it is not, as he is careful to note, because of the shortcomings of the available works *per se*, but because the human mind is not equally receptive, nor equally responsive, to the same stimuli. The implication is that the works on Jewish philosophy and ethics were useful for their time and age, or for the specific groups for whom they were written. Now there was a need for a new approach (in the light of the Chasidic doctrine), and for a "guide" that would command a universal appeal. However, the author realizes that even this book, in parts at least, cannot be so simple as to be understood by all. Consequently he urges the more learned not to be misled by a sense of misplaced modesty, and not to withhold their knowledge from those who would seek it from them in the understanding of these "Essays."[8]

Schneur Zalman knew his "perplexed" intimately. They flocked to him in great numbers, and they flooded him with written inquiries. Most of them, undoubtedly, were simple folk and laymen. But there were also many students of the Talmud, and philosophically inclined young men, who, like himself in his teens, sought a new way of life and new outlets for their intellectual as well as spiritual drives. The consideration of such a variegated audience largely determined the form and style of the book.

---

8. Ibid., p. 14.

IV

RABBI SCHNEUR ZALMAN'S philosophical approach may be defined as empirical and psychological. Rabbi Schneur Zalman based his approach on the principle of "From my flesh I see G-d."[9] His ethics is rooted in the unique nature of the Jewish soul, which is "verily a part of G-dliness Above."[10] In this respect, as well as in the special destiny of the Jewish people in the scheme of Creation, we find a close kinship between his approach and that of R. Judah Halevi, except that Halevi speaks for the Jewish nation as a whole, while Rabbi Schneur Zalman is more concerned with the individual.

The empirical approach, and the psychological method of inquiry, usually attempt to define religion by reference to that which is more certain than rational speculation, namely actual experience. It is the reflexive method of metaphysical introspection aiming at the development of the immanent realities and values leading first from G-d to man and then from man to G-d.

However, Rabbi Schneur Zalman's analysis of the nature of man is patterned after the Kabbalistic conception of G-d, in terms of the ten *sefirot*, *sechel* (intellect) and *middot* (attributes), which is the idea behind the Biblical declaration that "man was created in the image of G-d."[11] By applying these concepts and terminology to man first, they could be better understood in relation to G-d, an inverted method.

As to the ultimate objective of philosophical speculation, it will be illustrative again to draw a parallel between Maimonides' *Guide*, and Rabbi Schneur Zalman's *Tanya*. Maimonides' center of interest is to establish a true concept of G-d; hence his emphasis on the Divine attributes. Next in importance was to reconcile philosophy and religion, or faith and reason. The result was a compromise, which even at its best is not very satisfactory, for it entailed some concessions to reason at the expense of faith. This is why Maimonides' philosophical works aroused opposition in certain Rabbinic circles, and led an older contemporary of Rabbi

---

9. Job 19:26.
10. Job. 31:2. *Likkutei Amarim*, Part One, ch. 2.
11. Genesis 1:27.

Schneur Zalman, Rabbi Jacob Emden, to declare that "not the same man wrote both the *Guide* and the *Code*."

The basic problem, as Rabbi Schneur Zalman sees it, is this: Starting with the premise that there is a Creator and a transcendental and ineffable Deity, and on the further premise that unless the Creator could establish a rapport with His creatures, creation would be meaningless; and, finally, that rational man must be the vehicle of such a rapport—how are the finite and the Infinite to meet? How is the seemingly unbridgeable chasm to be bridged?

Rabbi Schneur Zalman's answer is as follows: Paradoxical though it seems—and the paradox is explained by means of the Lurianic doctrine of *Tzimtzum*—the finite has been endowed with an infinite, or transcendental, quality. In man it is the Divine soul which partakes in a real way of the nature of G-d. In nature, too, there are two sources of being: the immanent and transcendental, of which the latter constitutes true reality, whereby man can rise above his natural limitations, and establish communication with G-d. But, in accordance with the well-known adage that a man cannot raise himself by pulling at his hair, he has to find the means, outside and beyond himself, whereby to actualize his infinite potentials. This is where Divine Revelation, the Torah and *mitzvot*, serve as the central link in the *unio mystica* of man with G-d, through the Divine Law and precepts. For the Torah and *mitzvot* are the wisdom and will of G-d, and as in the case of the other two components, namely, G-d and man, the Torah too, in all its facets, possesses both revealed and esoteric qualities through which man's relationship with G-d is actualized and *unio mystica* achieved—a doctrine originating in the *Zohar*.[12]

This relationship is not confined to the mystic. Rabbi Schneur Zalman makes it his primary objective to bring this relationship within the experience of every man. With this in mind, Rabbi Schneur Zalman sets out to explain in rational terms, frequently by means of illustrations and analogies from daily experiences, the mystical and essentially supra-rational relationship between Creator and man. Although it has been said of the

---

12. *Zohar* III, 73a.

Tanya that its author had managed to compress the Infinite (*En Sof*) into a small book, Rabbi Schneur Zalman makes no attempt to use the method of the rational philosopher. Instead, he focuses attention on the infinite quality of man's potential, and on the infinite aspects of the Divine Law, with a view to bringing man into an intimate relationship with the *En Sof*, through the correlation of all three.

This brings us to yet another difference between the *Guide* and the *Tanya*, namely, in the concept of the Divine commandments and their essential function, particularly the so-called "supra-rational" precepts. To the *Guide* the ritual is primarily a means to attain true ideas that lead to a better understanding of G-d; to Rabbi Schneur Zalman it is an end in itself, as the vehicle of the highest degree of unity with the Infinite, for identity of will is more easily attainable than identity of thought. To the rational theologian, the so-called rational precepts, those which have to do with ethical and moral norms, are of primary concern; to the mystic who aims at *bittul*—the obliteration of the self—as a prerequisite to the highest level of *unio mystica*, the presence of human reason could be more of a hindrance than an aid, unless the so-called rational precepts are carried out with the same degree of *bittul* as the "supra-rational" ones. It is the latter which are more distinctively Divine.

Furthermore, ritual embraces things of nature, which, by being dedicated to G-d, are elevated and sublimated, thus transcending their physical limitations. Hence the cosmic importance of the ritual in reestablishing the Unity of G-d which was apparently (but not really) disrupted through the act of Creation.

V

THE PHILOSOPHY OF THE *TANYA* BEGINS WITH the self and ends with the self. Knowledge of the self, Rabbi Schneur Zalman holds, is a means to knowledge of G-d, the Creator, and also to knowledge of the created universe. However, methodologically speaking, the author starts with the self not so much from the viewpoint of the theologian or metaphysician as from that of the ethicist. His primary objective is to establish the absolute freedom of the human will. He further desires to establish that the human being is *essentially* a moral creature; moral, that is, not in some limited or conditional way, but fully and absolutely. Rabbi Schneur Zalman is a positive ethicist who believes that man has not only the fullest capacity for a perfectly moral life, but that its actual realization is within the possibility of the average individual. However, in order to be able to meet the moral tests facing the individual at every step of his daily life, the individual must be intimately aware of the psychic forces which motivate his dispositions and actions, and, above all, he must be convinced of his inherent moral strength.

With this in mind, our author proceeds to develop his elaborate structure of human psychology, the basic elements of which are derived from the Kabbalistic concepts of the human soul. His doctrine of the "two souls"—the Divine soul and the animal soul—enables him to establish absolute moral freedom on the basis of the absolute transcendency of the "Divine soul" in man. To the "animal soul," which is the vital principle of the physical body, the author ascribes all the natural dispositions inherent in man as a creature of this world. These are not evil in their pristine state, but rather neutral forces which, ideally, are to serve as the vehicle for the Divine soul which must act through them. They incline towards evil, however, since the animal soul is naturally susceptible to temptation. Hence the inner tension which man experiences in his daily life. But this tension between the two souls does not constitute a basic dichotomy in human nature, because the two souls stand in relation to each other as that of horse and rider. So long as the animal soul serves as the vehicle for the Divine soul, as it is meant to do, there is complete unity and harmony; the moment the animal soul acts independently, the harmony is disturbed. To the extent that the animal soul is permitted to assert itself, the human being acts from a "spirit of folly" which temporarily eclipses his Divine soul.

As Rabbi Schneur Zalman sees it, the animal soul has been given the power to challenge the authority of the Divine soul, but only for the purpose of evoking in the latter its fullest resources to overcome the challenge and be strengthened in the process. The individual must constantly be on the alert not to yield the slightest ground to the animal soul, since any such weakness would make the person increasingly vulnerable to the forces of temptation besieging his nature as a human being living in a material world, where indulgence can only lead to more indulgence in the process of daily living.

Rabbi Schneur Zalman believes that the average individual has the moral strength, if he but make the necessary effort, to suppress and hold in check those discordant forces, even if he may not be able to eradicate them completely. Consequently he is confident that personal harmony can be achieved, at any rate, in the whole area of the actual and practical moral life.

Rabbi Schneur Zalman's confidence in man's moral strength goes beyond the conviction, which all moralists must share, that the spirit is intrinsically superior to matter; or that reason is stronger than temptation. Rabbi Schneur Zalman does not define the Divine soul merely in terms of reason. He assigns to it both intellectual and emotional qualities (*sechel* as well as *middot*). The Divine soul is endowed with a "natural" or innate love and awe of G-d. This aspect of the Divine soul plays an important role in the ethical system of Rabbi Schneur Zalman. Clearly, the attainment of a moral life is much easier if, as the author holds, it largely depends on contemplative efforts to bring to the surface the natural love and awe of G-d already extant in the individual in a latent form, than if these motivating higher emotions had to be created anew by intellectual perception. In the latter case, moral life would be limited to a relatively few individuals with a high degree of intellectual insight, while Rabbi Schneur Zalman is concerned with bringing the moral life within reach of every individual.

Thus, the first and most elementary function of the intellect in Rabbi Schneur Zalman's ethics lies in *hitbonenut*—contemplation. Rabbi Schneur Zalman is a great advocate of periodic and sustained meditation. He repeatedly urges us to take time out to think. Moreover, as a teacher and mentor, and in this capacity he sees himself first and foremost, Rabbi Schneur Zalman goes to great length to provide also a syllabus of contemplation, as it were. He counsels us to dwell on the beauty and sublimity of the good, rather than on the baseness of evil, emphasizing the

11

rewarding experience of the holy deed. In this emphasis on the positive there is a certain deviation from the homiletics of the *Mussar* movement, which aims at the attainment of an ethical and moral life by accentuating the baseness of sin and its dire consequences and fostering a greater measure of asceticism.

Keenly aware of the frailty of human nature, the gravitational pull of the natural propensities, and the potency of the forces of temptation besieging the average individual in his daily life, the author is nevertheless convinced of man's ability to attain mastery of the self, in thought, speech and action. In *hitbonenut* the author sees the antidote to the "spirit of folly" which is behind every immoral act.

VI

ON A HIGHER LEVEL, HOWEVER, the intellect has an even more important function. Rabbi Schneur Zalman insists that the religious life cannot be complete without *hasagah*—intellectual comprehension of the nature of G-d, His Unity, Providence, and other fundamental principles of the faith. He recognizes, of course, that the degree of intellectual comprehension and perception differs in different individuals, but he insists that every person must strive for *hasagah* to the fullest measure of his capacity. In this Rabbi Schneur Zalman makes a significant departure from other Chasidic schools, notably the Polish and Galician Chasidim, who remained closer to the Beshtian approach. The latter gives predominance to *devekut*, emotional attachment in religious experience based on pure and simple faith. As we had occasion to note,[13] a leading contemporary of Rabbi Schneur Zalman strongly objected to his emphasis on intellectual inquiry, seeing in it a potential source of detraction from simple faith.

It may be added parenthetically that these Polish and Galician Chasidim are sometimes described as "ChaGaT" Chasidim, in distinction from "ChaBaD" Chasidim; "ChaGaT" representing the emotional qualities of *chesed*, *gevurah* and *tiferet* which they emphasize in preference to "ChaBaD," the intellectual faculties of *chochmah*, *binah*, *da'at*.

---

13. Mindel, *Rabbi Schneur Zalman of Liadi*, Vol. 1, p. 189 ff.

Rabbi Schneur Zalman certainly does not belittle *devekut*, but to him *devekut* without *hasagah* could be only of an inferior order. The *devekut* in Chabad is of a richer and deeper dimension, stemming from the higher forms of awe and love which are fostered by *hitbonenut* and *hasagah*.

No less important in the Chabad system is the intellect's function as controller of the religious emotions. The ideal servant of G-d in Rabbi Schneur Zalman's religious discipline is the individual who in his dedicated service (which to our author comprises every aspect of the daily life) attains the proper balance between cold reason and impassioned emotions. To use the Chasidic terms mentioned earlier, "ChaGaT" without "ChaBaD" is partial service, at best, and is apt to be distorted as well; while "ChaBaD" without "ChaGaT" is sterile speculation, hence of little value to Rabbi Schneur Zalman.

The place which Rabbi Schneur Zalman assigned to the intellect in the religious life, and his insistence upon the proper balance between intellect and emotion, had their effect on Chasidic thought as a whole. There can be no doubt that he had a considerable influence in tempering the excessive religious emotionalism which had been engendered in certain Chasidic quarters when the movement was still in its early stages of development.[14]

Being firmly rooted in traditional Judaism, Rabbi Schneur Zalman is committed to the basic view of historic Judaism which values knowledge primarily as the basis for action. Where Rabbi Schneur Zalman differs from his predecessors is in approach and method. There is a cardinal difference, for example, between the rational approach of Maimonides' *Guide* and the quasi-rational-quasi-mystical approach of the *Tanya*, a difference which, as we had occasion to note, often leads to significant differences in concept and emphasis. Yet, while noting some of the coincidences and divergencies of these viewpoints, we should not overlook the fact that the philosophy of the *Tanya* is in many respects complementary to that of the *Guide*. Rabbi Schneur Zalman often takes up the discussion where Maimonides leaves it, by introducing new insights borrowed from the *Zohar*, Lurianic Kabbalah, and other Kabbalistic and Chasidic sources.

---

14. Ibid., p. 44.

Rabbi Schneur Zalman does not engage in polemics with the classical Jewish philosophers. In his view, however, their religious philosophy must be supplemented by the many insights contained in the Kabbalah. In the *Tanya* itself there is little *direct* reference to Jewish philosophers and to the specific philosophical problems that occupied their attention. But in the *Shaar Hayichud v'haEmunah* and in his other works, Rabbi Schneur Zalman on occasion comes to grips with some of these problems, and his critique of the philosophical approach is more explicit.[15] However, it would take us too far afield to attempt here an analysis of this particular subject, which lies beyond our present study.

One general observation must be made in this connection. Speaking of the intellect and its functions in Rabbi Schneur Zalman's philosophy, it should be clearly understood that the intellect of which he speaks is not quite the same as that which was generally understood by the classical Jewish philosophers of the Middle Ages. The difference is in Rabbi Schneur Zalman's definition of the intellect. Having postulated that human activity is derived from two distinct sources, namely, the two souls, Rabbi Schneur Zalman also recognizes two intellects, the *sechel enoshi* (the "human" intellect inherent in the animal soul) and *sechel elohi* (the "divine" intellect inherent in the Divine soul). The first is unreliable in dealing with the absolute truths. It is completely enmeshed in the phenomenal world of the senses overshadowing the true reality of things. It cannot, of its own accord, disengage itself from the material world of which it is an integral part. Consequently, its discursive as well as its intuitive knowledge is fallible. The philosophers, according to Rabbi Schneur Zalman, proceeded entirely from this so-called *sechel enoshi*, which is the reason why their speculations could lead them to erroneous conclusions, such as misconceptions of the unity of G-d, or *creatio ex nihilo*, and similar truths,[16] which have

---

15. Cf, for example, *Torah Or* 6a; 14d; 15a; 42d. *Likkutei Torah, Vayikra* 6a; *Tazria* 19c; *Shelach* 50a; *Va'etchanan* 6a; *Drushim Lishmini Atzeret* 92b; *Shir Hashirim* 7d.

16. Rabbi Schneur Zalman makes no specific reference, but it seems that he has in mind the general polytheistic nature of Greek religion and the Aristotelian philosophy cited in the *Guide* of Maimonides.

been Divinely revealed in the Torah. It is from the latter that the *sechel elohi* derives its knowledge, whereas the knowledge that the *sechel enoshi* is capable of producing is "extraneous" knowledge, and its speculative sciences are "extraneous sciences" (*chochmot chitzoniot*). Hence the chochmot chitzoniot are "contaminated" and "contaminating" to the pure "divine" intellect.[17] Nevertheless, such knowledge, too, can be useful if it is applied to good advantage, "good" according to Rabbi Schneur Zalman's definition being that which is consecrated and subservient to G-d. On this basis Rabbi Schneur Zalman defended such Jewish philosophers as Maimonides and Nachmanides for engaging in *chochmot chitzoniot*.[18]

The *sechel elohi* alone is the source of true knowledge. Of its three faculties ("ChaBaD"), the faculty of *chochmah* ("wisdom") is the "point," i.e., fountainhead, of intuitive wisdom, the wisdom of G-d; it is also the point of *bittul* (*chochmah*—"*koach-mah*"), the recognition of the unreality of matter as perceived by the senses, including the complete suspension of the self and its merging into the Divine All. *Chochmah* thus conceived opens the gates of the intellect to true perception and comprehension, leading to positive knowledge (*da'at*). *Da'at* has a "binding" quality; it binds the *sechel* to the *middot*. By means of *da'at* intellectual perception ripens into feelings and actions. The whole intellectual process, as Rabbi Schneur Zalman sees it, begins with intuitive flashes of perception in *chochmah*, which flourish into mature ideas in *binah*; thence they are transformed by *da'at* into refined emotions and, finally, into motivated actions. When the *sechel elohi* thus illuminates and permeates the entire self, the *sechel enoshi* becomes refined and purified under this process, so that it, too, with its attendant *middot*, can participate in, and contribute to, the moral and spiritual fulfillment of the individual in a harmonious and complete measure. Herein, according to Rabbi Schneur Zalman, lies the key to the fulfillment of man's personal destiny.

---

17. *Tanya*, ch. 8; *Torah Or*, 41a. Cf. *Zohar* II, 124a.
18. *Tanya*, end ch. 9.

VII

FOR MOST ETHICAL PHILOSOPHERS, here would be the end of the road. But to Rabbi Schneur Zalman, as a mystic, this is but the first milestone, for personal destiny is linked with the destiny of mankind as a whole and with that of the universe. If the rational ethicist can say that the destiny of mankind as a whole is nothing more than the sum total of the individual destinies, and draw the line there, Rabbi Schneur Zalman, in the light of the Kabbalah, probes further. Human life, both on the individual and collective levels, cannot be considered apart from the universe in which it has its setting. If man has a destiny, it must be related, in some specific and intimate way, to the destiny of the world in which he lives, and of which he lives. It is from this point of view that our author inquires into the nature and reality of existence, and, specifically, in what way man's actions affect not only his own destiny but also the destiny of the universe as a whole. The final step in this reflective thinking is to relate both man and his world to the only true Reality, which, to Rabbi Schneur Zalman, is G-d.

Rabbi Schneur Zalman sees unity and harmony as the substratum of reality. The complexity of human nature parallels the multiplicity of things in Nature, but beyond the external images there is a transcendent unity, which is rooted in the all-embracing unity of the Creator. Nature, insofar as it participates in man's destiny, itself undergoes a process of refinement whereby it gradually fulfills itself. Its destiny will be fulfilled when it will have become so refined and purified as to no longer obscure its true reality, which is of G-d.

Thus moralist turns mystical philosopher as Rabbi Schneur Zalman unfolds his system, in which he seeks to establish the transcendency of human nature within a transcendent universe, and to show how both are mutually correlated and inter-related by means of the transcendent Divine Law, all working in unison towards the realization of their mutual destiny which is rooted in the mystic unity of the All in All.

As a mystic, by which we mean his identity with the Kabbalah, Rabbi Schneur Zalman has made several notable contributions to the mainstream of this Esoteric Discipline. He emerges not only as an important, and in many respects original, interpreter of the Lurianic school, but also as a rational exponent of the Kabbalah in general. By pouring many an abstruse Kabbalistic doctrine into rational vessels, he has removed much of the obscurity which had been attached to the Kabbalah, and has given it an acceptable place in Jewish religious philosophy.

Rabbi Schneur Zalman's ethical system basically rests on Kabbalistic foundations. Yet under his ingenious treatment, and by shifting emphasis from heaven to earth and from the afterlife to this life, including his effort to bring the Messianic ideal into the here and now, Rabbi Schneur Zalman presented us with an original ethical system. It is an attempt, as we have seen, to relate the totality of man, both on the individual and collective levels, to the totality of the surrounding world, and to correlate the whole order of things to the Giver of Life, in a positive and meaningful way. It is, moreover, a bold attempt to make this system accessible, in a greater or lesser degree, to the *benoni*, the "average" individual.

Rabbi Schneur Zalman's interest in speculative philosophy and speculative mysticism is mainly motivated by his primary concern with practical ethics. He seeks a unified *Weltanschauung* for its positive application in the daily life. The Chabad philosophy may well be described as an "ergo" philosophy, in the sense that it is interested in the *practical* conclusions rather than in the theoretical speculation for its own sake. In this sense the object of the *Tanya*, the "Written Law" of Chabad,[19] in relation to which all the rest of the Chabad literature is but commentary, seems to be to formulate a way of life rather than a school of thought. In effect, however, it has achieved a large measure of both. In the realm of Jewish thought, one of Rabbi Schneur Zalman's main contributions, in final summation, lies in his effort to effect a harmonious synthesis of the main streams of Jewish thought, the Halachah, Kabbalah, and *Chakirah* (Jewish religious philosophy), in which the practical, mystical and rational aspects of Judaism are harmoniously integrated and blended.

---

19. *Kitzurim v'Ha'orot l'Tanya*, by Rabbi Menachem Mendel of Lubavitch, ed. Rabbi M. M. Schneerson (Kehot, 1948), p. 118 f.

"Chabad," as a school of thought as well as a way of life, is the result of this mystico-rational interpretation of Judaism, and while it is not quite original in some of its elements, it is yet quite new in its synthetic composition as a whole.

As for the creator of this system, it is in the pattern and fabric of his system, and in the unity and comprehensiveness of his outlook, that we shall find the dimension and depths of his thought.

Chapter I

THE HUMAN PERSONALITY

The Two Souls

We have already had occasion to note[1] that Rabbi Schneur Zalman begins his ethical work with an analysis of the psychological composition of the human—more specifically, the Jewish—personality. As a practical ethical philosopher and moralist, his immediate concern is with the psychic forces which mold the pattern of the daily conduct of the "average" individual.

Thus, in the very first chapter of the *Tanya*, the author lays down the foundation of his psychological system, which is based on the doctrine of the "two souls." These souls are conceived as the sources of all human activity, and of the conscious and unconscious forces behind them.

The first is the so-called "animal soul" (*nefesh habahamit*). It is the vital principle that animates the physical body, the "life" of the body. Indeed, it is also called the "vital soul" (*nefesh hachiyunit*), and the author uses the two terms interchangeably and, frequently, conjointly: "the vital animal soul" (*nefesh hachiyunit habahamit*). It is the source of the bodily instincts and appetites and from it the senses derive their perception. The "vital" soul in man is akin to the "vital" principle that animates all created beings, inasmuch as it is the principle of their existence and functions. For this reason the mineral, vegetative and living forms of

---

1. Mindel, Introduction, *Likkutei Amarim* [*Tanya*], Part One, pp. xxv, ff.

19

existence are said to possess a "vital" soul. But in addition to its animal functions, the vital soul in man possesses certain essential qualities, such as intellectual and emotional attributes, which are not to be found in the lower animal species, and which make the "animal soul" in man distinctly "human." These would include self-esteem, pride, modesty, ambition, and many other dispositions, both good and bad, which are "natural" to most men, and which come under what is commonly called "human nature."

The second soul is of an entirely different category. It is defined as "a part of G-d above indeed,"[2] and termed the "Divine soul" (nefesh ha'elohit). It is completely independent of the body in the sense that it exists before its coming into the body, and it survives the body after the latter's death. The Divine origin of this soul provides the extra-mundane dimension which enables the soul, while residing in the body and animal soul, to rise above them and act in defiance of the natural dispositions of the individual.

In other words, Rabbi Schneur Zalman presupposes two *distinct sources* of human activity: one *natural* and *this-worldly*; the other *supernatural* and *other-worldly*, and in his terminology—the "animal soul" and "Divine soul," respectively. These two sources are combined in the living individual.

The doctrine of the "two souls" provides the basis for a number of interesting deductions, the most significant of which may be summarized as follows.

The complexity of human dispositions, especially the commonly experienced conflict between that which one is *disposed* to do and that which one knows one *ought* to do, does not stem from the division between the body and the mind, as had been assumed by some psychologists of the Middle Ages. In some Medieval analyses of human psychology, particularly those following the Neoplatonic tradition, the body, as the vehicle for the lower faculties of the soul, was blamed for the evil impulses in man's life, which man shared with the lower species. The rational faculties alone, namely, the intellect and rational will, were believed to be uniquely human. Consequently, a moral life could be attained only by the mastery of the mind over the body, i.e., by the morti-

---

2. *Tanya*, beg. chap. 2.

fication of the flesh. Moralists held that such mastery was possible because they believed that the mind was independent of the body, and that the rational contents which constituted the mind did not arise within, nor were they a real part of, the impulsive life.

In Rabbi Schneur Zalman's analysis, however, the human being is not simply a being composed of a body and a mind, but of a body and *two* minds, since each of the two souls has a mind of its own, with a will and reason of its own. The animal soul is the source of intellectual perception which is limited to the individual's *natural* mental capacities; the author calls it the "human intelligence" (*sechel enoshi*). This "human" intelligence manifests itself in such activities as the sciences, arts, handicrafts, and the like. The Divine soul, on the other hand, is the source of a higher, or "Divine intelligence" (*sechel elohi*). The "Divine" intelligence manifests itself in the quest for knowledge of the Creator, in love and awe of G-d, in the sense of the sublime and the holy, and in concern with similar purely spiritual matters.

Inasmuch as the animal soul is concerned with mundane matters and is the source of the instincts and impulses, its mind, will and reason are all influenced by the nature of this animal soul, since they arise within, and are part of, this animal soul. In this case the mind and the body act in unison, and there could be no freedom of will in a moral sense. It is only by virtue of possessing at the same time also a Divine soul, which is "other worldly" and which transcends the body with all its dispositions, that man truly has freedom of choice in his actions.

As for the body itself, with all its natural dispositions, it need not at all be assumed that it is bad, any more than nature at large may be assumed to be bad in a moral sense. In Rabbi Schneur Zalman's analysis, the body is neutral ground, an instrument which can be used for either good or bad. Moreover, the very natural dispositions themselves are innocent forces which can be debased or sublimated at will.

The two souls, as conceived by Rabbi Schneur Zalman, do not constitute a dichotomy in the strict sense. The animal soul and the Divine soul do not reside in the body side by side, as two separate and irreconcilable entities. Rather are they closely interlocked, with the Divine soul informing the animal soul and acting through it, while both together inform the body and act through the bodily organism. Nevertheless, they are distinct in their essence, being derived from two distinct sources, and this distinction provides the polarity of dispositions in human experience. It is the Divine soul, however, which constitutes the true essence of the human being. The Divine soul is the unifying principle which is potentially capable of making the individual a whole and harmonious man. Indeed, on balance, the Divine soul is potentially the stronger of the two, standing in relation to the other as light is in relation to darkness. Where light and darkness meet, light must prevail as a matter of course. In Rabbi Schneur Zalman's view there is no doubt but that the human being is essentially a moral creature.

Rabbi Schneur Zalman's doctrine of the "two souls," as he indicates in the opening chapter of the *Tanya*, is based on R. Chaim Vital,[3] the exponent of Lurianic Kabbalah, and is loosely related to a Scriptural text.[4] Rabbi Schneur Zalman develops it at great length, and makes it a corner-stone in his ethics, philosophy and mysticism. He gives us a detailed analysis of the nature and functions of each of the two souls, which will be summarized below.

The Divine Soul

THE "DIVINE" SOUL (*nefesh elohit*) is conceived as a substance which is "a part of G-d above, indeed." Its relationship to its Maker is based on more than a vague spiritual affinity. Rabbi Schneur Zalman sees the soul as emanating from G-d. To describe the soul's close relationship to its Maker, the author draws a parallel between the descent of the soul from the Divine Mind and the physical process of procreation, whereby a child "evolves from the paternal drop of semen deriving from the paternal brain."[5] Thus, the Scriptural text, "Ye are children unto the Lord your G-d,"[6] is to our author more than a figure of speech, or an

---

3. *Shaar Hakedushah* and *Etz Chaim*, Portal 50, ch. 2.
4. Isaiah 57:16.
5. *Tanya*, chap. 2.
6. Deuteronomy 14:1.

expression of endearment. The relationship between the Divine soul and its Heavenly Father is more real to him than the corresponding blood relationship in the physical world. For, whereas in the physical world a father and son constitute two separate entities, the Divine soul and its Heavenly Father are never detached, since in the metaphysical order there are no limitations.[7]

The concept of such an absolute affinity has far-reaching implications, not only for the man-G-d relationship, but also for the inter-human relationship. It lends reality to the Chabad concept of true brotherhood. For although the author acknowledges that there are myriads of gradations in the quality of souls, he insists, nevertheless, that all emanate from the Supreme Mind, or Supernal Wisdom (Chochmah Ila'ah), and all thus truly have one Father. Hence, those individuals who are conscious of possessing such a soul must be conscious of the close affinity that unites them with others. It is only such individuals who accentuate the physical and material aspects of life that see themselves as separate bodies. But, after all, it is the spirit and not the body that constitutes the essence of man, and those who, like Rabbi Schneur Zalman, can see through the outer shell and perceive things in their true essence and reality, must be conscious of unity rather than separateness. This feeling of real brotherhood is not restricted, of course, to the Chasidic community.[8]

Turning to the nature and faculties of the Divine soul, Rabbi Schneur Zalman develops an elaborate anatomy of the psyche.

He, too, speaks of the psychic triad, the nefesh, ruach and neshamah. But in the Tanya this triad is not conceived in terms of faculties distinct from the soul's substance, as in Platonic thought, but rather in terms of the soul's substance.

What exactly is meant by the triple distinction of nefesh, ruach and neshamah, as conceived by Rabbi Schneur Zalman, is not explained specifically in the Tanya. Apparently, the definition of these terms is of no immediate concern to the main theme

---

7. Cf. R. Isaiah Hurwitz, Shnei Luchot Habrit (Amsterdam, 1698), pp. 326b; 380b.

8. See Abraham H. Glitzenstein, Rabbi Yisrael Baal Shem Tov, (Kehot, 1960), pp. 154 ff. Rabbi Schneur Zalman's doctrine of Ahavat Yisrael is completely influenced by the Baal Shem Tov's teachings.

of this work, which, as we had occasion to note, centers on Divine service reaching to the highest levels of love and awe of G-d. However, from other sources where Rabbi Schneur Zalman deals with the subject, we gather that the said three categories of the soul are conceived as three dimensions of the soul's essence itself. Broadly speaking, it may be said that *neshamah*, the highest dimension, is reflected in the soul's intellect powers; *ruach*—in its emotion powers; and *nefesh*—in the soul's outer manifestations, or "garments," namely, the faculties of thought, speech, and action. Be it as it may, the *nefesh*, *ruach* and *neshamah*, "constituting the Divine soul even of the *amei ha'aretz* and the most worthless, all emanate from the Supreme Mind, which is, as it were, the Supernal Wisdom (*Chochmah Ila'ah*)";[9] all belong in the higher source of consciousness and have nothing to do with the lower instinctual or impulsive life, which lie within the realm of the animal soul. Rabbi Schneur Zalman's concept of the soul as being composed of *nefesh*, *ruach* and *neshamah* is largely derived from the *Zohar*, where all three are conceived as being already contained in every soul.[10]

The soul operates by means of its *powers* which in turn are manifested through the bodily organism. The *Powers of the Soul* (*kochot hanefesh*) are divided into two broad categories: General Powers and Particular Powers. The *General* powers are Delight (*oneg*) and Desire or Will (*ratzon*).[11] They are termed "general" because they are not associated with any specific organ of the body. One may find delight in intellectual activity, or in emotional experience, or in the activity of any of the physical organs. Similarly, the desire and will exercise influence over the intellect and emotions, as over the conscious movement of the bodily organs.

The *Particular* powers are subdivided into two categories: Intellect-powers (*sechel*) and emotional qualities (*middot*). The Intellect-powers are said to "reside" in, i.e., act through, the brain, whence they extend to the heart. From their primary seat in the brain, the intellect powers extend to other bodily organs by means of the nervous system, such powers manifesting them-

---

9. *Tanya*, chap. 2.
10. *Zohar* I, pp. 79b, 141b, 206a; III, 70b, etc.
11. The Hebrew word *ratzon* means both desire and will.

selves in various skills and arts performed by the bodily organs.

The intellect has three faculties: *chochmah*, *binah* and *da'at* (hence the abbreviation ChaBaD). These are generally translated as "wisdom," "understanding," and "knowledge," respectively. But in the *Tanya* these terms mean something quite different. What is meant here by *chochmah* is the power of conception, the faculty where an idea is first conceived; *binah* refers to the cogitative faculty, where the idea is analyzed; and *da'at* represents the final state in the mental process, where the idea attains its most definite comprehension, which, in turn, gives rise to corresponding emotions and feelings. *da'at* is the mental faculty that transforms ideas into motivated dispositions.

Chochmah is creative; *binah* is developmental; *da'at* is concluding. The conclusion produced by *da'at* will vary with the type of subject engaging the mind: in theoretical speculation it will produce the logical inference or opinion, e.g., the verdict in a legal problem; in moral judgments it will produce a disposition consonant with the judgment, such as a feeling of attraction or aversion in relation to the moral issue under consideration. It is with the latter function of *da'at* that our author is specifically concerned.

Creative intellectual activity begins with a "flash," or a "point" (comparable to the geometric point that is the beginning of all construction). The Hebrew word *chochmah* contains the letters that can be reconstructed to form the two words *koach-mah* ("the potential what").[12] Undefined and inarticulated, this "point" already contains the whole concept *in potentia*, like a seed potentially containing the whole tree with its fruits. Because it is as yet amorphous, comprehension is lacking, and the flash of illumination might be dissipated unless it is promptly developed. Here it is where the faculty of *binah* takes up this "point" and begins to expand it. The idea begins to take shape and form, depth and breadth. The "point" develops into a structure. (*Binah* comes from the root *banah*, to build.)

In the mystic language of the Kabbalah and Chasidut, *chochmah* and *binah* are termed "father" and "mother," because *chochmah* impregnates *binah* and from the union of the two the

---

12. *Tanya*, chap. 18. The faculty of *chochmah* is identified with humility and self-abnegation (*bittul*). Cf. *Zohar* III, p. 34a.

higher emotions are born.[13]

However, even after the idea is conceived and developed, it might still remain in the abstract, in the realm of pure speculation, unless the mind becomes completely imbued and thoroughly saturated with it, producing mature conviction and total commitment. This is the function of the third faculty, *da'at* "knowledge," in the Biblical sense of the word, as in "And Adam knew Eve,"[14] in the sense, that is, of attachment and union, resulting in a close correspondence between the intellect and the emotions.[15]

The faculty of *da'at* is of especial importance in Rabbi Schneur Zalman's psychological system. It is not only the concluding phase of the reasoning process, but also that intellect-power which exercises control over the consciousness; it compels and concentrates attention on the ideas arising in the mind. *Da'at* is the link between the reason and the emotions, and since the steadfast occupancy of the conscious mind is the prime mover of the higher emotions, and the latter in turn determine action, *da'at* has a decisive and dynamic role in determining the whole personality of the individual.

The intellect-powers of the Divine soul manifest themselves in contemplation of the Divine Being, of the *En Sof*. The emotions which these intellect-powers produce are fear, or awe, of the Divine Majesty, specifically the dread of being separated from G-d; and love of G-d, namely, the desire to be attached and united with Him. Love and awe are the primary emotions, from which all others evolve.[16]

In addition to the three intellect-powers, the Divine soul possesses seven essential affections, or emotional qualities (*middot*). The Hebrew word *middot* means "measures," and the emotions (or affections) are so termed because they vary in quality and intensity in accordance with the quality of the intellect-powers of the individual which produce them.

The first three emotional qualities are the principal ones.

---

13. *Tanya*, chap. 3. Cf. *Zohar* II, pp. 85a, 290a.
14. Genesis 4:1. Cf. *Shnei Luchot Habrit*, op. cit., p. 149b.
15. *Tanya*, chap. 3.
16. Ibid.

They are *chesed* ("kindness"), *gevurah* ("severity," in the sense of restraint), and *tiferet* ("beauty," in the sense of harmony). The next three—*netzach* ("victory"), *hod* ("splendor"), *yesod* ("foundation")—are secondary and auxiliary. The seventh, called *malchut* ("majesty") is the outlet through which all emotions are communicated.

Chesed (kindness) is an affection which manifests itself in the outpouring of benevolence. It finds expression in charity, sharing of knowledge and in all acts of love and goodness. It is, in fact, identified with the primary emotion of *love*. It knows no limits.

Gevurah (severity) expresses itself in contraction, constraint, withholding. It is related to the primary emotion of *fear* (or awe).

Tiferet (beauty) is a synthesis of the first two, with *chesed* predominating; a moderated kindness, resulting from the interplay of *chesed* and *gevurah*.

Kindness by itself, unlimited and untempered, despite its apparent attractiveness, can be self-defeating and harmful. Too much love spoils the child; too much bounty can be corruptive.

To be fully effective, the attribute of kindness must be tempered with that of severity, limiting the endowment to the absorptive capacity of the recipient. The injection of severity into kindness produces a new quality called *gevurah shebechesed* ("severity-in-kindness").

Severity unmitigated is clearly undesirable. It must be tempered with kindness. This quality is termed *chesed shebigevurah* ("kindness-in-severity"). An obvious example of it is found in the disciplinary action of the parent chastising the child.

The other emotional qualities, too, are not to operate in their pristine states, but must combine with one or more of the others, according to prevailing circumstances, or the needs of the situation. The initial combinations of the emotional qualities with each other result in 7 x 7, that is 49, affections or dispositions.

The three intellect-powers together with the seven emotional qualities are said to correspond to the ten supernal *sefirot* whereby G-d manifests Himself in Creation.[17] In fact, just as the human soul descended from its Divine origins, so are its ten powers descended from the ten Divine Attributes. For it is a basic

---

17. Ibid., beg. chap. 3.

27

principle in Chabad, as in Kabbalah in general, that all phenomena in the temporal world have their "source" and origin in the eternal order.

In addition to these ten powers, the soul is said to possess three auxiliary instruments as outlets for its creativity. These are *thought*, *speech* and *action*. They are termed "garments" of the soul, being external to it. Thought is the instrument of the intellect. It is more closely related to the soul and enjoys a greater unity with it than the other two.[18] It is continuous in its action, being constantly fed by an endless flow from the infinite capacity of the soul's intellect.

Speech and action are more properly the auxiliaries of the emotions, since the latter necessarily exist in terms of an external object and must be communicated.

In thought itself there are said to be three categories, corresponding to the three faculties of the intellect, *chochmah*, *binah* and *da'at*, mentioned above. In the first, the thought is in its pure form, unarticulated. In the second, the idea receives mental "verbalization." Here we find the term "letters of thought." In the third, the thought has fully matured and seeks actual expression.

Having defined this soul as a part of the Divine, it is to be expected that all its powers would be oriented toward G-d. The nature of this soul is such that by its very essence it knows no commitments save to G-d alone. Its interests and activities are wholly centered on G-d. Its essential attributes are awe and love of G-d; it desires only obedience to G-d and communion with Him. In the light of the above, Rabbi Schneur Zalman goes on to define the three "garments" of the Divine soul, namely, thought, speech, and action. These, too, are Divine in nature, being the soul's contemplative, verbal and actual activity centered on the Divine Wisdom and Will which are embodied in the Torah and its precepts. These "garments" are thus the vehicles whereby the Divine soul communes with its Maker.[19]

---

18. Ibid., chap. 8.
19. Ibid., chap. 4.

The Natural Self

TURNING TO THE "ANIMAL" SOUL, Rabbi Schneur Zalman affirms that it is in all respects the counterpart of the Divine soul. Like the Divine soul, the animal soul comprises ten powers, three intellect-powers and seven emotion-powers, with the latter predominating. But in contrast to the ten powers of the Divine soul which descend from, and reflect, the ten *sefirot* of holiness, the powers of the animal soul descend from, and reflect, the ten *sefirot* of unholiness, the so-called "ten crowns of profanity," emanating from the *sitra achra*, the "other side," i.e., not the side of holiness.[20]

In the *Tanya* and Chabad literature, the concepts of the *sitra achra* and of the *kelipot* ("husks," or "shells") lose much of their dark and sinister aspects with which they are associated in Kabbalah. In a more rationalistic way, Rabbi Schneur Zalman defines these evil forces in terms of separateness, in contrast to the forces of holiness which are those of unity. Rabbi Schneur Zalman's conception of Creation, and the appearance of evil, will be discussed more fully later. For our present purpose it may be summarized as follows.

The whole created order, on its various levels, from the highest to the lowest (i.e. down to our material world)—as Rabbi Schneur Zalman sees it—constitutes a hierarchy of worlds that come into being, on various gradations, by the creative process emanating from G-d. This will be better understood by recourse to the oft quoted principle, "from my flesh I visualize G-d," in terms of the human counterpart. Suppose an idea occurs in a person's mind. It first develops into a concept, which is as yet on a purely intellectual level. Then comes the desire to express it, i.e., the idea descends into the realm of emotion. Next, the faculty of thought takes up the idea as to the ways and means of expressing it. Having been formulated in thought, the idea descends into the realm of speech, in actual articulation. Finally, the person writes the idea down on paper, or proceeds to implement it otherwise in actual deed. The idea is present in all those stages, but on different levels, going through a process of "descent" or "materialization."

---

20. Ibid., chap. 6.

In a somewhat similar way creation is to be understood as a "descent" from the first Source, giving rise to a series of worlds, from the most sublime to the progressively more "material," as they are further "removed" from their Source. This process produces in the created beings a state of "separateness" from G-d. The degree of materialization and separateness, of which the created beings become aware, increases with their distance from the source of their emanation. Those beings which are nearest to their source retain a higher degree of coalescence and unity; those further removed from their source receive a greater measure of independence and separateness. At the lowest stage of this process of emanation, there emerges a realm of almost complete separateness. This realm is called *sitra achra* (the "other side"). It is inhabited by existences which are termed *kelipot* ("shells"), because in them the Infinite Light which had brought them into being is completely eclipsed by their outer "shell."

This concept of creation in terms of separateness provides Rabbi Schneur Zalman with the basis for his doctrine of evil. All evil is derived from, or related to, the *kelipot* and *sitra achra*. Moral evil is any action characterized by separateness from, or disobedience to, G-d.[21]

There are two categories of *kelipot*. At the extreme end are the so-called "three unclean *kelipot*," which are completely "dark" and evil, and have no good at all; and there is the "translucent *kelipah*" (*kelipat nogah*), which is on the borderline between the side of holiness and that of the "other side." The *kelipat nogah* has an admixture of good in it, though inherently it inclines towards the other *kelipot*. Correspondingly, in the sphere of morality, there is a sort of a "neutral" category to which belong actions that are neither good nor bad. For example, acts of benevolence which are performed not in obedience to the Divine Law, but simply out of a compassionate nature, would belong in this category. Where such benevolent acts are tinted with outright selfish motives, however, they belong in the category of the "three unclean *kelipot*," and are intrinsically bad.

The animal soul of the Jew, Rabbi Schneur Zalman declares, is derived from this *kelipat nogah* described above. Hence it pos-

---

21. Ibid., chaps. 7, 22, 37, 40.

sesses some good qualities, namely, the *natural* traits of compassion and benevolence. But predominantly it is concerned with itself and with the needs of the body. Where it is allowed free play, its intellect and its affections, expressed through its three "garments," namely, thought, speech and action, are all self-centered and this-worldly; they constitute "all the things which are done under the sun, which are vanity and a striving after the wind," or "the ruination of the spirit."[22]

Here we have a startling innovation. According to Rabbi Schneur Zalman, all the good and noble traits of which a Jew prides himself, such as compassion, benevolence, modesty, etc., in fact any and all of the cardinal virtues, are not always expressions of the Divine soul. If they are stimulated *naturally*, they merely reflect the inherent good qualities of the animal soul! Only if they are practised in direct response to the Divine commandments, out of a pure sense of obligation and duty, are they true moral qualities resulting from the assertion of the Divine soul. As for the majority of mankind, Rabbi Schneur Zalman takes a very dim view of the moral quality of man's good deeds, since they are almost invariably tainted with selfishness.[23]

The "seat" of the animal soul is said to be in the heart, more specifically in the "left ventricle of the heart," whence it extends by means of the blood circulation to the other parts of the body, including the brain. That is why all the lower emotions are said to arise in the heart.[24] By contrast, the Divine soul is said to reside primarily in the brain, whence it extends to the other parts of the body, including the heart, specifically the right side of it.[25] In other words, the higher emotions are primarily intellectual. Thus, by extension, one may say that there can be a conflict between the heart and the mind. But this is only a figure of speech, since, as already explained, there can be no conflict on physiological grounds. The real cause of the conflict, in the view of Rabbi Schneur Zalman, lies in the two sources of consciousness, or, in Rabbi Schneur Zalman's terminology, in the tension between the

---

22. Ibid., chap. 6.
23. Cf. R. Bachya ibn Pakuda, *Duties of the Heart*, chap. 5.
24. *Tanya*, beg. chap. 9.
25. Ibid.

two souls, the Divine and the animal. In this conflict the body itself, with all its physical attributes, is the *neutral* battling ground,[26] a "no-man's land," so to speak, for the complete possession of which the two souls are constantly fighting, each endeavoring to make the body and all its limbs a "vehicle" for its ten faculties and three "garments" to the exclusion of the other's.[27]

While, generally speaking, in the case of two contending parties, peace may be achieved by the complete surrender of either adversary to the other, this is not so in the case of the inner human conflict. Here only one resolution of the conflict can bring about true peace, harmony and unity, namely, the victory of the Divine soul over the animal soul, that is, the victory of the forces of good over the forces of evil in man's nature. The Divine soul may be temporarily eclipsed and subjugated, but it will never surrender completely. Its "small, still voice" may be stifled, but never stilled. Its surrender would cry out against the whole order of things, against the whole scheme of Creation, where the good is destined to prevail, because it is intrinsically the superior of the two, inasmuch as the existing order must vindicate itself as a good order, created by a benevolent G-d. On the other hand, where the tide of the battle turns in favor of the Divine soul, and the animal soul is held in check, or, as in rarer instances, completely vanquished, real peace, harmony and unity can be achieved.

The Benoni

IT SHOULD BE NOTED THAT in the view of Rabbi Schneur Zalman the so-called animal soul, with all its self-centered interests and dispositions, is not evil in itself. Man is, after all, a natural creature who could not survive without his natural dispositions and instincts any more than any other living species. One cannot speak of the lower species as being good or bad simply because they are guided by natural dispositions and instincts. The human being, however, is different because he is subject to temptation and excessive indulgence, in a manner which is unknown in the

---

26. Cf. Duties of the Heart, chap. 3.
27. *Tanya*, chap. 9.

lower animal kingdom. It is the *abuse* of his natural dispositions, not the dispositions themselves, which makes them bad.[28] However, as will be seen later, these "innocent" dispositions, too, must be sublimated to the service of G-d, as otherwise they would retain an element of evil in that they remain in the realm of the animal.

We are thus introduced to another category in the animal soul, the tempting imagination, or the "evil inclination" (*yetzer hara*). As Rabbi Schneur Zalman conceives it, it is a force, or a drive, within the animal soul, and which is fed by the latter's passionate nature, and in turn excites that nature.[29] The *yetzer hara* is the inseparable companion and ally of the animal soul. They act and react upon each other constantly, that is to say, the animal soul produces natural dispositions, which the *yetzer hara* fosters and fans into passionate appetites and excessive cravings. If these are indulged in, they debase the animal soul and accustom it to an ever-growing variety of desires, more tainted and corrupt and more intense. This makes the work of the *yetzer hara* easier, and so the vicious circle grows. Unless the appetites can be held in check, the individual is likely to become a thoroughly immoral person.

To offset the *yetzer hara*, the Divine soul is said to be endowed with a "good inclination" (*yetzer tov*), which is sometimes identified with "the still, small voice" of the conscience. Its nature is

---

28. This is, of course, the traditional view of Judaism, dating back to the Sages of the Talmud, who generally held the physical body in high esteem, and were opposed to excessive mortification of the flesh, or any form of monasticism. *Bereshit Rabbah*, chap. 9:7; *Brachot*, 9:1.

29. In one passage of the *Tanya* (chap. 29, p. 37a), the *yetzer hara* is identified with the animal soul. However, it is evident from other passages that the author does not identify the two, but that the *yetzer hara* is a power distinct from, though connected with, the animal soul. In his *Torah Or*, p. 28, Rabbi Schneur Zalman defines the *yetzer hara* as a power stemming from the affections (*middot*) of the animal soul, and like the latter is not essentially evil but rather a neutral driving force; hence it lends itself to sublimation. This view is implicit in the Talmudic statement (*Brachot*) referred to in the previous note. It should be noted, however, that we find different views in the Talmud and among Jewish thinkers on the *yetzer tov* and *yetzer hara*. Some regarded them as angels, others as spiritual powers arising in the soul and body, respectively. See also *Guide*, part II, chap. 6.

intellectual, deriving its strength from the Divine soul, which is primarily intellectual.

In any conflict between desire and duty, these auxiliary forces, the *yetzer hara* and *yetzer tov*, are in the forefront of the inner struggle, but behind them are the animal and Divine soul, from which the respective natural disposition and the sense of duty derive their impetus.

Using the classical metaphor,[30] which sees in the human body an embattled "small city"[31] for the conquest of which two implacable kings are waging relentless war, the author proceeds to evaluate the two conflicting forces stemming from the two sources of consciousness.

Both antagonists are fighting for total victory. The interests of the animal soul are concerned with the physical senses and emotions, that is, with the gratification of the appetites. It seeks to capture the entire mind and body, so that they become a "vehicle" for it, to be directed and driven at its will, with the individual's every thought, word and act serving the animal soul only.

The Divine soul likewise seeks to capture the "small city" to the total exclusion of the animal soul, so that the individual's every thought, word and act be dedicated to G-d. More than that, it seeks to conquer and convert the animal nature in man, so that those very passions which are directed towards the sensual and physical, may be completely reversed and directed toward a passionate love of G-d. Using the same metaphor, it may be said that not only does the Divine soul desire to capture the "small city," and to rule it, while keeping the opposing force at bay, but it desires to incorporate the opposing force in its ranks, thereby augmenting its own forces.[32]

What is more, the opposing force, in the author's conception, is inwardly prepared to "desert," as it were, the animal soul and join forces with the Divine soul on its march to victory. Such a complete surrender is not possible, if victory is on the other side. The Divine soul would never acquiesce in defeat.

The reason why complete resolution of the conflict is possi-

---

30. *Nedarim* 32b.
31. Ecclesiastes 9:14
32. *Tanya*, chap. 9.

ble only in one direction is, the author tells us, as follows: The animal soul is not an end in itself, for man was not created for the purpose of striving to become an animal. Its ultimate function, apart from informing and animating the physical body, is, by its very opposing nature, to serve as an instrument of the Divine soul. It is a function which combines various aspects, not the least of which is to provide a contrast, as by way of illustration, darkness intensifies the light when the darkness is illuminated, or thirst intensifies the pleasure to be derived from refreshing water. It serves as a challenge to bring out the best and utmost in the Divine soul. Furthermore, it is a potential reservoir of emotional powers upon which the Divine soul can draw every time the latter prevails. For, as has been noted, the strength of the animal soul lies in its passionate nature. If it can be harnessed in the service of the Divine soul, the latter could attain a greater intensity of passionate love for G-d than it can of its own accord, since its own nature is primarily intellectual. Metaphorically speaking, the animal soul stands in relation to the Divine soul as the draft animal to man. When the beast is yoked, man's productiveness increases many-fold, and, moreover, the beast fulfills its highest function. Indeed, the metaphor is drawn from the Scriptural text, "there is an abundance of produce by the strength of an ox."[33]

The crucial point, however, is that true to its nature and function the animal soul inherently "desires" to be vanquished and transformed, for its task is to tempt, but not to seduce.[34] Here the author draws upon a parable in the Zohar[35] which illustrates in bold strokes the "mission" of the animal soul.

A king desired to test the moral strength of his only son. He engaged a most charming and clever woman to seduce the crown prince. Explaining to her the purpose of the test, the king bade the "harlot" use all her charms to beguile his son, yet without betraying in any way her mission. Any shortcoming on her part, he said, would ruin the test, and her failure would be tantamount to disobedience. Should the prince acquit himself well in the test, a reward would await both him and the "harlot." The "harlot's"

33. Proverbs 14:4.
34. *Tanya*, end chap. 9.
35. *Zohar* II, p. 163a.

duty is merely to tempt the prince, not actually seduce him. Thus, while she must use all her seductive powers, she must inwardly desire that the prince should not succumb to her "charms."

Place the lower passions of the animal soul in the position of the "harlot" and we get an insight into the author's conception of moral evil.

At the root of this conception is an optimistic view of human nature. The inner conflict is very real; temptations and passions are very strong; but it is not a meaningless, nor a hopeless, struggle in which man is engaged. With all their apparent reality, the forces of evil are inherently conquerable and, what is more, even convertible to good.

The outcome of this conflict depends entirely on man, for he is equipped with a superior intellect to cope with it. The manner in which a person acquits himself in this conflict will reveal his personality, which may fall into any one of five broad types.

At the beginning of the list is the perfectly righteous person (tzaddik gamur). He is one who has succeeded not only in overcoming temptation, but also in sublimating his nature and converting it to good account. As a result, he is so fully and completely permeated with the love of G-d, that this love is matched only by his abhorrence of evil.[36] He belongs to the elite, the "superior men, whose numbers are few."[37] Their activity is of the highest cosmic importance: they "transform evil into good, darkness into light, bitterness into sweetness,"[38] thereby causing Divine influence and benevolence to flow unhindered; they are instrumental in reaffirming the Divine Unity in the physical world. We have here the daring doctrine that man—the tzaddik gamur—can "benefit" G-d, as it were.[39]

However, Rabbi Schneur Zalman often emphasizes that man's ability to "benefit" G-d is not confined to the tzaddik gamur. Each mitzvah fulfilled, each good deed performed, regardless of the personal status of the individual, has a similar effect,

---

36. Tanya, chap. 10.
37. Ibid.; Sukkah 45b; Sanhedrin 97b.
38. Zohar I, p. 4a.
39. A doctrine derived from Tikkunei Zohar, as stated in Tanya. chap. 10.

except that when it is performed by the *tzaddik* it is, of course, on the highest level.

This doctrine is further expanded by Rabbi Schneur Zalman into an important aspect of man's service to G-d, wherein "kindliness" to G-d serves as a distinct motivation, in addition to love and awe. We have in mind the attribute of *rachamim* ("mercy") which, in Rabbi Schneur Zalman's system, is the third component of the three main dimensions of Divine service (love, awe, and mercy), as will be developed later.[40]

The next type is that of the *tzaddik she'eno gamur*, the imperfect *tzaddik*. He falls short of the perfect *tzaddik* only insofar as he has not achieved complete abhorrence of evil. The natural temptations and passions have not been completely eradicated and sublimated, and whatever residue of them is left in him prevents his love for G-d from being as complete, overwhelming, and ecstatic as in the perfect *tzaddik*. But such evil as still remains in his system is so minute as to be of no real consequence. In this class there can be many gradations, depending upon the quantity and quality of the residue of evil still latent in his nature.[41]

At the lower end of the scale are the two types of wicked men (*rasha gamur* and *she'eno gamur*). The completely wicked man has completely lost his "small city" to the forces of evil; there is no good left in him, or, in common language, his conscience bothers him no more.

Nevertheless, the Divine "spark" in his soul is not extinguished even in such a person. It is in a state of "exile" or peripheral existence, outside his consciousness. This is why even the completely wicked person may, albeit on rare occasions, be reawakened to do *teshuvah* (repentance), even to the extent of complete transformation. However, until this happens, he is completely submerged in evil. Such a type is fortunately rare. More prevalent is the "not-completely wicked man." He is one who actually succumbs to temptations and moral relapses, which are intermittent with regrets and repentances. Here, too, there can be many gradations depending upon the frequency of the moral relapses and to what extent the "small city" is captured by

---

40. See p. 98 f. below.
41. *Tanya*, chap. 10.

the evil forces, whether in the way of a sinful thought, word, or act, or in all three of them. But the "still, small voice" has not been completely stifled. Having gratified his desire, he will experience a strong feeling of remorse, yet he is too weak to overcome temptation when it presents itself again. Not so the completely wicked. In him all good has been dislodged. Yet, even the completely wicked man is not given up as a lost cause. According to our author, the good with which every person is originally endowed, lingers on even in the completely wicked, in a sort of peripheral way; it is ineffective but not dead; it is rather in a state of suspended animation.[42] This is what makes it possible, though it is very rare, for even a completely wicked man to experience a radical transformation or conversion.

In between these two extreme types of good and wicked men is the intermediate class, the personality of the *benoni*, on whom our author focuses his greatest attention.

The *benoni*, the "intermediate"[43] personality, is our author's favorite concern. He believes, moreover, that to be such is within the practical grasp of everyone.[44]

As the author defines the term,[45] the *benoni* is not one whose good and bad deeds are in equilibrium. A person who alternates between good and bad has already been defined by the author as a wicked man, and included in the category of *rasha she'eno gamur* ("incompletely wicked"). The *benoni* never consciously commits a sin, nor succumbs to temptation. The animal soul in him, strong as it may be, never gets to a position of control. Its three outer "garments," namely, thought, speech, and action, find no accomplice in the body. These outlets are firmly and permanently held under the sway of the Divine soul, which means that the *benoni* never commits the sin of entertaining an evil thought, or uttering a bad word, or commiting an immoral act. Yet he is not

42. Ibid., chap. 11.
43. The term "*benoni*" is discussed in the first chapter of the *Tanya*, and is borrowed from the Talmud (*Brachot* 7a). Rabbi Schneur Zalman gives it his own definition and meaning, from which it becomes apparent that he also had in mind the *benoni's* peculiar function as an "intermediary" between the Creator and the creation, as will be revealed in the course of our discussion.
44. *Tanya*, beg. chap. 14.
45. Ibid., chaps. 1, 12, through 15.

called *tzaddik*, because the supremacy of the Divine soul over the animal soul in the *benoni* is confined to the three outlets only, but does not extend to the essential ten faculties.[46] In other words, in the *benoni* the animal soul is held on a leash; its desires and lusts are effectively controlled, but not sublimated. Consequently he is subject to temptation. However, if the *benoni* appears at first glance as a "split personality," in whom both natures, the good and the bad, seem to have an equal voice, this is of no practical consequence. For, in effect, the conflict is but momentary, and is *invariably* resolved in favor of the Divine soul, since the latter is irradiated with the Divine Light, and where light and darkness clash, darkness must give way to light.[47] We say "invariably," because this is implied by the very definition of the *benoni* as one who never *actually* commits evil. Should he fail to repress an evil thought, word or act, he at once forfeits his status of *benoni* by the terms of definition. In the *benoni* the animal soul is strong enough to challenge, but not actually to contest, the Divine soul, and challenge it does relentlessly.

The *benoni* is thus destined to experience a continuous inner tension, which is relieved only during propitious moments of inner harmony, such as during prayer, when the animal soul temporarily becomes completely overwhelmed and submerged. During sincere and ecstatic prayer, the animal soul is mesmerized, as it were. All thoughts of the flesh are banished during these periods of communion, when the animal soul lies "dormant."[48] But no sooner does the *benoni* return to his daily pursuits than the animal soul awakens and the person may again become acutely aware of cravings and temptation, and he must bend every effort towards repressing them. And repress them he can, since "the head is, intrinsically and innately, master over the heart."[49] For, as the author frequently reminds us, the superiority of the Divine soul over the animal soul is like the superiority of light over darkness. A little physical light dispels a great deal of darkness; the

---

46. See p. 33f. above.
47. *Tanya*, chaps. 12, 13.
48. Ibid., chap. 13.
49. Cf. *Zohar* III, p. 224a; ibid., *Ra'aya Mehemna*, p. 233b ("the brain is 'water'; the heart—'fire.'"). Cf. *Shnei Luchot Habrit*, p. 9b.

darkness must simply give way to light. Similarly, the irradiated Divine soul dislodges the animal soul and checks it effectively, permitting it no expression in thought, word, or act.[50]

It is noteworthy that the *benoni* is credited with complete self-control not only in relation to his speech and actions, but also thought. By "thought" the author means the conscious activity of the mind, when its attention is captured and held by some idea or image so that it becomes a part of one's experience. The author recognizes that the *benoni* is vulnerable to strong instinctive stimuli which, by their appeal to any of his congenital impulses, are likely to excite his involuntary attention. But it is up to the individual to determine how much, if any, conscious attention the idea will receive from his mind. He may dwell on it, or immediately dismiss it. It goes without saying that a great deal of effort is required to dismiss a persistent or exciting idea, but the *benoni* is capable of it. In other words, he may not be able to prevent a sinful thought from entering his mind, but he must not willingly dwell on it for one conscious moment; he has the power to divert his attention immediately to something else, even to something diametrically the opposite.[51]

It can be seen that the *benoni* of the *Tanya* is on a considerably higher plane than the *tzaddik* of the Talmud, where the term is used also in reference to one whose meritorious deeds outweigh his transgressions, while the *benoni* is defined as one whose good deeds and bad are in equal proportion.[52] As our author defines the *benoni*, he is one who never actually commits a sin, though he may be tempted to, for he is always in full control of his thoughts, words, and actions and consistently resists temptation. But this high status notwithstanding, our author unequivocally declares that the level of the *benoni* is one to which everyone should aspire and which is, indeed, within everyone's reach. For the *benoni* is required to do nothing but to exercise self-control. He is expected to "turn away from evil" and to "do good," and herein every person has been endowed with complete freedom of choice,

---

50. *Tanya*, chap. 13. Note there the author's interpretation of the concept of "Divine aid" in the victory of the good over evil.
51. Ibid., chap. 12.
52. *Rosh Hashanah* 16b; cf. also *Brachot* 7a.

40

as well as with the capacity to carry out his determination "not to be wicked even for one moment."[53] Were he required to abhor evil in his heart—that would have been beyond the capacity of the average person; that is the realm of the *tzaddik*. The *benoni*, however, is only expected to recognize his human weaknesses, fight to overcome them, and do so with confidence, in the knowledge that he has the powers to overcome them. The author concedes that it is not an easy task. It requires constant vigilance, and one must, at least occasionally, aim at the higher target of training oneself to abhor evil, and striving for joyous and ecstatic communion with G-d, in order to assure that he will at least not fall short of the *benoni* category.[54]

The inner conflict which the *benoni* experiences is not equal in all *benonim*. There is the person who is by nature more phlegmatic, less given to temptation and lust; there is the assiduous student who is not so exposed to temptation. There is even the person who has cultivated good habits to the degree where they have become second nature to him. But unless he exerts himself *over and beyond* his nature, innate or acquired, he cannot truly be called a servant of G-d, for he is serving his own nature rather than G-d. The *extra* effort, giving of himself just a little more than he is wont to do, is the real test of Divine service.[55] Hence, the ideal of the true Divine servant is not to attain a state of static behavior, however good it may be; it is a dynamic and conscious effort to transcend himself, and achieve absolute mastery over his nature and habits. The good and the holy must always be on the ascendancy.[56]

---

53. *Tanya*, chap. 12.
54. Ibid., chap. 14. This is something of a concession, since Rabbi Schneur Zalman does not generally encourage the idea of dwelling on evil. However, even here he hastens to mitigate this "concession" by urging meditation on the opposite, by way of contrast. Note it there.
55. Ibid., chap. 15.
56. This is an example of a Halachic law (*Brachot* 29a; *Menachot* 99a) not related to ethics, being applied by Rabbi Schneur Zalman as a moral principle.

CHAPTER II

THE COSMIC ENTITY

Two Sources of Being

Rabbi Schneur Zalman's analysis leads him from the human personality to the world, which he views as a cosmic entity, and from there to the problems of relating both to the Divine Being.

To Rabbi Schneur Zalman, as to all Kabbalists, man with his physical and spiritual powers is a replica of the *Adam Kadmon*, the Primordial Man, the first manifestation of the Divine Image, the source of all creation. The *Adam Kadmon* is the spiritual arche-type of the mystical "organism" first emerging from the hidden G-d in the act of creation. The human soul that irradiates the human organism and constitutes its true essence is a reflection of the Light of the *En Sof* that pervades the *Adam Kadmon* and the whole cosmic order, constituting its true reality and unifying principle. Likewise all the powers of the human soul, *oneg*, *ratzon*, *sechel*, and *middot*, discussed in the previous chapter,[1] are derived from their supernal proto-types. Therefore, if we want to know something about the ultimate reality of the world we live in, and how G-d the Creator manifests Himself through this reality, we must begin with a study of the human being.

Rabbi Schneur Zalman conceives of the whole created order as one entity. We have seen that, according to Rabbi Schneur Zalman, the human personality is two-dimensional. Man possess-

---

1. See p. 24ff. above.

42

es two levels of consciousness, a "natural" and "supernatural." Consistent with this idea, Rabbi Schneur Zalman believes that the cosmic entity likewise partakes of two sources of being. This accounts for the two-dimensional nature of everything in the phenomenal world, as can be seen on various levels. On a lower level we have, for instance, the distinction between matter and form, or between a thing and its properties. On a higher level, we have Nature as a whole and the Laws of Nature. On a still higher level, we conceive of the universe, in its entirety, as a single entity, with a "soul" which constitutes its true reality.[2] Rabbi Schneur Zalman goes further and affirms that the cosmic entity, like the human personality, seeks fulfillment. In the human being the quest for fulfillment may be conscious or unconscious; in the cosmic entity it could only be unconscious, but in other respects the two are identical. The significance of this doctrine for Rabbi Schneur Zalman's ethical system will become apparent in due course. Let us first examine the two sources of being of which the cosmic entity is said to partake. This must be preceded by a few words on the symbol of "light" as used by Kabbalists in reference to creation.

The reason for this metaphor is easy to see if we consider some of the properties of light. Light is the most subtle and abstruse of all physical phenomena. It is the most immaterial of physical things; it is the borderline between the material and immaterial. Light is energy; it is the source of existence and life. Light is sensible only when it is reflected in material objects. There is visible and invisible light. Light has a transcending quality; it penetrates all places alike and illuminates all things indiscriminately without itself being affected or soiled. A beam of light can be screened and infracted without affecting its source of radiation. It ceases when its source is shut off and can therefore exist only in conjunction with its source. All these qualities, and more, are applicable to creation. Rabbi Schneur Zalman has made ample use of these categories to bring the idea of creation closer to understanding.

Creation begins with the Light of the *En Sof* (*Or En Sof*), which in the process of radiation from its Source goes through

---

2. Cf. *Guide*, part I, chap. 72.

various stages of transformation and condensation, as it were, until, in the final stage, it is reduced to a finite, indwelling force in nature, combined with an infinite force which transcends the universe. The transition from the infinite to the finite, and the creation of existence which partakes of both, is explained by the doctrine of *tzimtzum*, which will be discussed later. Here we need concern ourselves only with the end product of this creative process, our two-dimensional world.

The two sources of being from which the cosmic entity partakes are termed *sovev* (or *makif*) and *memalei*, which literally means "surrounding" and "filling," respectively, or, in more familiar terms, transcendent and immanent. These two sources, conceived of as an extension of the creative Light of the Infinite (*Or En Sof*), constitute the constant preserving force of all existing things, hence the true reality of all existence. Inasmuch as light has no existence apart from its source, the *En Sof* must constantly act through the *Or En Sof* in order to create, preserve, and vitalize all things in existence. It is in this ultimate sense that one can speak of G-d as being both immanent and transcendent in the created world.

The doctrine that G-d is in some inexplicable way both immanent and transcendent with respect to the world is, of course, not new, nor are the terms *sovev* and *memalei*. In fact, both terms are already found in the *Zohar*.[3] Maimonides regarded the transcendence and immanence of G-d as a "complete mystery."[4] Our author does not hesitate to probe into this mystery. The limits of our comprehension, Rabbi Schneur Zalman held, stretch beyond the line drawn by Maimonides and philosophers in general, thanks to the new insights provided by the Kabbalah, especially in its Lurianic development.[5] Our author develops this

---

3. *Zohar* III, *Ra'aya Mehemna*, 225a.

4. "How G-d rules the earth and provides for it is a complete mystery; man is unable to solve it. For, on the one hand, it can be proved that G-d is separate from the universe, and in no contact whatever with it; but, on the other hand, His rule and providence can be proved to exist in all parts of the universe, even in the smallest. Praise be He Whose perfection is above our comprehension." *Guide*, part I, chap. 72 (M. Friedlander's translation, p. 119).

5. See "Note," beg. of chap. 2 of *Tanya*. Cf. also *Torah Or*, 42d; *Likkutei Torah*, *Va'etchanan* 6a; *Shir Hashirim* 7d.

idea further, and in his characteristic way pours its mystic content into a more rational vessel. Moreover, he held that not only is comprehension of this creative process accessible to our mind, but that such knowledge was necessary in order to understand our place in the world we live in. Contemplation (*hitbonenut*), which plays a very important part in his system (and he never tires of recommending it),[6] is, in fact, directed toward this subject; a subject, be it noted, which he recommends not for philosophers alone, but for the average individual, the *benoni*.

The phenomenal, sensible world, Rabbi Schneur Zalman explains, derives its reality from the Divine emanation termed *memalei*. In this form the emanation from the Infinite Light comes down in such a "contracted" and "reduced" form as to be capable of being "clothed," or confined, within finite objects. This is the so-called *giluy or*, the "revealed" form of the Infinite Light, which is manifest in creation itself and in the vitality of the created things in their finite state. It is so "reduced" as to bear no comparison with, or relation to, the "concealed" Light (*or ganuz*) which retains its infinite quality and does not become incorporated in the finite worlds, but "surrounds" them peripherally, as it were, being beyond their apprehension; hence it is called *sovev* or *makif*. For example, considering our global earth, we can conceive the Divine factor in it in its power to produce minerals and vegetation, but this is but an infinitesimal fraction of the creative force—the Infinite Light—which has brought the earth into being, of which we can have no notion at all.[7]

The term *makif* ("peripheral") should not, needless to say, be understood in any literal sense, for that would imply a limitation in space; it is to be understood as a force that transcends and, at the same time, pervades all created things through and through, thereby serving as their real source of continuous existence.

Empirically, the concept of transcendency can be illustrated by the mind's transcending capacity in the act of comprehension. When a person recollects something which he had seen, or reflects on something which he is seeing, that thing being fully grasped in his mind and thought, the mind is said to comprehend

---

6. Cf. *Tanya*, chaps. 3, 14, 16, 23, 25, 29, 31, 33, 41-43, 46, 48.
7. Ibid., chap. 48.

or "encompass" that thing. The thing is, of course, independent of man's thought, and is not affected by it in any way. Here the simile ends, for G-d's thought and knowledge of the thing surround and penetrate its every atom *in reality* (unlike man's grasping a thing only in his imagination), and it is this Divine knowledge which is the very life and existence of the thing, constantly creating it thereby out of nothing.[8] But since this force is infinite, it could not in its pristine state create a finite object; hence it is "projected" through the "contracted" form of the Infinite Light, so that the *sovev* (or *makif*) and *memalei* act in unison to create finite objects. The combination of the two forces is often described as an act of "clothing," viz., the *sovev* is "clothed" in the *memalei*, the latter being the "garment" which conceals the former. The two forces are inseparably interlocked; they are simultaneously derived from the same source in the Infinite Light, and each, in conjunction with the other, is responsible for the existence of the revealed and hidden aspects, respectively, of all created things.

Thus the doctrine of the two-dimensional creative force provides an explanation for the two dimensions of physical things— viz., matter and form, which in the human being correspond to body and soul. Matter and form are inseparable in sense experience, since both together, in union with each other, invariably constitute every thing in the "sensible" world. But were we able to imagine the material substance of a thing as separated from its form, we would say that the substance of the thing comes into existence by the Divine force termed "*sovev*" or "*makif*," whereas its form comes into existence by the Divine force termed "*memalei*," as will become clearer in subsequent discussion, in the following pages.[9]

The variety of things in our material world is primarily due to the variegated manifestation of the immanent aspect of the *Infinite Light* in the material things surrounding us. In general, all things in our physical world are divided into four categories, or "kingdoms": inorganic matter, vegetation, animal life, and man. (This is also the order of creation in the first chapter of the Book

---

8. Ibid.

9. The subject is discussed more fully in *Torah Or*, on *Megillat Esther*, pp. 92b ff.

of Genesis.) This gradation marks the order of things according to the relative manifestation of the creative force in them.[10] The scale is determined by man's intellectual apprehension and sensory perception of the manifest "vitality" of things. One can discern the greatest degree of creativeness in man, the most intelligent of all creatures, and least of all in inorganic matter, which *apparently* has no life at all. However, "dead" matter is not considered dead in Lurianic Kabbalah; it, too, is considered to have a "soul"; this soul is the *koach hapoel banifal*, the "creative force in the created thing," which keeps everything in continuous existence, and which is the *real* "life" of the thing. It is synonymous with the "word" of G-d, whereby everything came into being.[11]

However, the above gradation and order does not reflect the true reality of things. In nature the higher forms of life are sustained by the lower: plant life is nourished by inorganic matter; animal life is sustained by both, and man lives off all three lower "kingdoms." If the lower forms of life did not contain something which was lacking in the higher forms of life, how could the lower sustain the higher? Our author deals with this question more explicitly elsewhere,[12] but for the sake of completeness this problem must receive some attention here.

The explanation is based on the doctrine that behind the physical forces of nature there are, as stated earlier, spiritual forces which are the real source of their existence. These spiritual forces are in turn sustained by the Divine Light and Life vested in them, i.e., in the "transcendent" and "immanent" forces that are contained in all things. These two creative forces, Rabbi Schneur Zalman explains, interact in all things in an inverted ratio. The greater the immanent vitality of a thing, the lesser is its station in the transcendental order; conversely, the more primitive or corporeal a thing is, the stronger is the transcendent force that permeates it. This theory is linked with Luria's doctrine of the "Breaking of the Vessels," to which our author refers only in passing,[13] and hence may be omitted from our present discus-

---

10. *Tanya*, chap. 38.
11. *Shaar Hayichud v'haEmunah* (Part II of *Tanya*), chap. 2 ff.
12. *Iggeret Hakodesh* (Part IV of *Tanya*), chap. 20.
13. *Tanya*, chap. 8; *Iggeret Hakodesh*, chaps. 26, 28.

sion. Suffice it to say, that it is based on the principle that "that which is highest falls lowest," so that inorganic matter, the "lowest" in the order of creation, retained a "spark" in the primordial act of creation which has its origin in the highest spheres. In this sense our author interprets the Scriptural text, "Not by bread alone doth man live, but by everything that proceedeth out of the mouth of G-d doth man live."[14] This means that it is not the physical bread that sustains man, but the "word" of G-d contained in it, namely, the spiritual force which endows the earth with the capacity to produce bread through a process which is itself a form of *creatio ex nihilo*; the "word" of G-d, that is, which enables such a thing as bread to exist after it had not existed, and which constantly keeps it from reverting to non-existence; that is what sustains man.[15]

Thus, the four kingdoms can be graded in two opposite directions: On the rational level, it is a gradation on the ascent, i.e., from inorganic matter upwards to man; and on the mystic level it is graded on the descent, from inorganic matter downwards to man, inasmuch as the Divine "spark" in inert matter is in some respect of a higher order.

The Transcendental Order

NOW, WHAT HAS BEEN SAID of the natural yearning of the Divine soul to unite with its Maker is true, we are told, also of the Divine "spark" which sustains all things, and which is the "soul" of all things, as stated above. This "spark" also constantly seeks to unite with its original "flame," as a small flame is drawn to, and absorbed in, the bigger flame. As a result there is a continuous process of "ascension," whereby inorganic matter (water, soil, minerals) is transformed into vegetation; vegetation into blood, tissue, and bone of animals; and the dumb animals into the "speaking" animal. So great is the urge for this spiritual "fulfillment" that physical laws are defied in the process, as, for example, when minerals and water are drawn upwards in plants and trees reaching great heights, etc., in an apparent defiance of the law of gravitation.

---

14. Deuteronomy 8:3.
15. Mindel, *The Commandments*, Kehot, 1966, p. 29 ff.

To the mystic these phenomena have a simple explanation. All things flow from the Creator, all things exist and live by Will of the Creator, and all things strive to return to the Creator in order to be "dissolved" in the Source of their reality.

In this eternal quest for reality our author sees the underlying principle of the whole creation. The mystic order of creation is a complete circle, starting in G-d and ending in G-d, thus fulfilling the mystic unity of creation with Creator.

But this unity cannot be attained without human intervention. Man holds the key to its fulfillment. The three other "kingdoms" can rise no higher than man. Man alone can rise and unite with the Infinite, and thereby raise the other three "kingdoms" which sustain him, so that through him they are also absorbed in the Infinite. If, however, man makes pleasure the end of his pursuits, following the dictates of his animal soul, he fails in his function. In such a case the upward trend is arrested, and the mystic cycle is broken. Moreover, not only does man, in such a case, fail to unite the creation with the Creator and elevate the entire creation, but he even degrades it, especially when he transforms the energy derived from the other three "kingdoms" into immoral acts, which they could not otherwise "commit."

Thus man is given a far-reaching destiny in the cosmic order. Of all creatures, man alone is conscious of the fact that there is a mysterious scheme in creation. Man, and only man, feels the summons of the Infinite and is free to heed or ignore it. Man is therefore the link between heaven and earth, the "fuse" that completes or cuts off the circuit. The very nature of man, possessing a Divine soul and an animal soul, makes him an admirable intermediary between the material and the spiritual, and the force whereby the physical is transformed into the spiritual.[16]

In the light of the above, it is clear why man's actions are considered of such cosmic importance. In the conquest of himself, by subjugating his lower nature and harnessing the passions in the service of G-d and the fulfillment of the Divine Will as expressed in the religious precepts and good works, man conse-

---

16. It would not be presumptuous to suggest that the author's commitment to the doctrine of man's "intermediacy" in the scheme of creation was a factor in the title of his work *Sefer shel Benonim*. See note 43, previous chap.

crates his entire being, thereby elevating his surrounding physical world. For, inasmuch as man derives his physical energy from the lower three "kingdoms," the spiritualization of his energy means the spiritualization of his physical environment. Herein lies the mystic significance of the fact that most of the 613 commandments of the Torah are performed by means of material objects, involving a mineral, vegetable or animal product, whereby the Divine "spark" which is held "captive" in them is "released" through the performance of the religious act. By means of these religious acts, not only are the material things spiritualized, but the Infinite Light is, at the same time, diffused in the physical world, and the material shell, the *kelipah*, is dissolved in the comprehensive unity of the All. Multiplied by all the individuals performing the precepts, the entire physical world constantly undergoes a process of sublimation and spiritualization. The "screens" that obscure the Infinite Light in our world of the senses gradually fall off. Our sensory perception and intellectual apprehension are being purified simultaneously with the purification of the gross material world surrounding us. In due course this process will be completed, and then the full glory of G-d will be revealed even to our senses, which will have attained their acme of perfection. Apprehension of the Divine Being will then be at its highest, something in the nature of the prophetic experience of the Revelation at Sinai. But whereas that experience lasted only for a fleeting moment, the people being unable to endure it and therefore obliged to request the intermediary office of Moses,[17] the revelation of the future will be without "screens" or intermediaries, as the people will have been "conditioned," as it were, to behold the Infinite Light without expiring or dissolving in the intense Light.[18]

With the "redemption" of the holy from the profane (in *kelipat nogah*) and the consequent separation of the good from the evil, not only is the good "elevated," but *ipso facto* the evil is dissolved and abolished. For evil can exist only as long as it has an admixture of good in it, or is indirectly "nourished" by good. Stark evil, in all its nudity, has no existence and no reality of its

17. Exodus 20:19.
18. *Tanya*, chap. 36.

50

own; hence it will be eradicated in the Seventh Millennium, when the physical world will attain its ultimate perfection.[19]

Such, in brief, is the author's application of the doctrine of *tikkun* ("reparation") which is of crucial importance in Lurianic Kabbalah.[20] Rabbi Schneur Zalman makes it the substratum of his ethical system. The Divine soul is pure and sinless and requires no *tikkun* in itself.[21] The purpose of its descent into the physical world is to "repair" the animal soul and physical body which it is sent down to inhabit. By bringing the latter under its sphere of influence, the Divine soul attains personal harmony and unity, and fulfills its personal destiny. This fulfillment has a two-fold aspect. Subjectively, the soul attains a higher degree of perception into the G-dhead through its religious experience in the fulfillment of the Torah and *mitzvot* during its earthly life. Objectively, the fulfillment of the personal destiny is linked with the destiny of the world as a whole, since it contributes its share towards the restoration of the cosmic unity (*tikkun ha'olam*) and the eventual establishment of the Kingdom of Heaven on this earth.

Unity As A Problem In Ethics

WE HAVE SEEN THAT Rabbi Schneur Zalman's philosophy begins with the self. Knowledge of the self, he held, was antecedent to knowledge of the Creator and the created world. But his main interest in the self was not so much from the viewpoint of the theologian as from that of the ethical philosopher. His first objective was to establish that man is endowed with absolute freedom

---

19. Ibid., chap. 37.
20. The doctrine of *tikkun*, in its original sense, has to do with the primordial act of creation. It is already alluded to in the Aggadic statement: "(Said G-d), If I create the world in the attribute of judgment—*din*—it could not survive; if I create it in the attribute of mercy, it could not survive. I will therefore create it in the combined attributes of judgment and mercy." *Bereshit Rabbah* 12:15; *Pesikta Rabbati* 40. Similarly in Rabbi Abahu's statement, "Before creating this world, G-d created (many) worlds and destroyed them, saying, 'Those did not please Me,'" etc. *Bereshit Rabbah* 3:9; *Zohar* I, 24b. Luria developed this doctrine in conjunction with his doctrine of the "breaking of the vessels," and the transition from the world of *Tohu* to that of *Tikkun*, as will be discussed elsewhere.
21. *Tanya*, chap. 37.

of action, since he holds that no ethical system can really be valid without this fundamental principle. Rabbi Schneur Zalman established man's freedom of will on the basis of the doctrine of the two souls. Man's real self, Rabbi Schneur Zalman holds, namely, that which distinguishes him from the lower species, is not his physical or mental qualities, but his spiritual quality, the so-called Divine soul. Since this soul is other-worldly and super-natural, it is not subject to the laws of nature. Man is, conse-quently, basically absolutely free.

The next step was to determine the ethical criterion, or first principle, by which actions and ends were to be judged. How is goodness and badness to be defined? What constitutes a good act and what is a reprehensible one? Here, too, Rabbi Schneur Zalman's position is clear and categorical. To Rabbi Schneur Zalman goodness is related to holiness, that is, to G-dliness. The good and holy is that which directly stems from G-d. It is identi-fiable with the will of G-d. A good act must be a holy act, for it must be consecrated to the will of G-d. It may be asked, What is the will of G-d? But that presents no problem at all to Rabbi Schneur Zalman. G-d's will, insofar as man is concerned, has been revealed in the Torah, the Written as well as the Oral Law.

By the same principle, a bad act is an act that is not dedicat-ed to G-d. A good act is an act *towards* G-d; it strengthens the process of reunification with G-d both on the individual level as well as on the universal level. A bad act is an act *away* from G-d; it intensifies disunity within the individual and within the universe at large. Good is unity, evil is separateness, disunity.

It is from this point of view that Rabbi Schneur Zalman takes pains to explain, in as simple terms as possible, the concept of the unity of G-d.

The problem of the unity of G-d is intimately connected with the question of creation, namely, whether the universe came into being by a process of creation *ex nihilo*, or whether it always existed. The ancient Greek philosophers did not conceive of any-thing being created "out of nothing." Jewish tradition, on the other hand, maintains that the world was created out of nothing and created in time. To be sure, the finite human mind is inade-quate to grasp the doctrine of *creatio ex nihilo*. Such ideas as finite things coming from the Infinite, matter from the Immaterial, plurality from the One, to mention some of the integral components of the said doctrine, are hard to conceive by the created, hence limited, human mind, in view of the fact that such phenomena are simply outside of human experience and beyond human ken. Yet, these are Divinely revealed truths, regardless of human comprehension.[22] Nevertheless, Rabbi Schneur Zalman attempts to bring this doctrine, too, closer to our understanding. To him it is basically a question of the immutability of G-d: the difficulty of comprehending the idea that G-d could have created the world without it causing any change in Him. He felt that if one could explain, in approximate terms at least, how the creation of the world did not affect a change in the Creator, the unity of G-d would be upheld, and all other pertinent problems would likewise find a rational solution.

The Kabbalists, especially R. Moshe Cordovero, attempted to find a solution to this problem by means of the theory of an intermediate agency, the *sefirot* (emanations). But the basic difficulty still remained unresolved, for the principle of intermediate agents applied by the Kabbalists was, in effect, the same as applied by some philosophers, primarily Maimonides, except that the latter used somewhat different terminology, calling them "Spheres" (*galgalim*), Intelligences, Angels, and the like.[23] The difficulty is not with the principle itself, but with the assumption that creation came into being by a process of cause and effect, the Creator being the First Cause. This, in Rabbi Schneur Zalman's view, was the stumbling block of the philosophers, as well as of the Kabbalists preceding R. Isaac Luria. For, inasmuch as there is an affinity between cause and effect, the interposing of any number of causes and effects between the First Cause and the last, would not remove the difficulty. It was not until R. Isaac Luria introduced the doctrine of *tzimtzum* that a new way was opened

---

22. It should be mentioned, in passing, that the alternatives to *creatio ex nihilo* entail far greater difficulties, as well as contradictions; which is the reason why so many different, and often contradictory and mutually exclusive, theories and hypotheses have been offered on the question of the origin of the universe. However, this is not the place to examine them.

23. Cf. *Guide*, part II, chaps. 4 through 12.

to a re-evaluation of the problem of creation, of the unity and immutability of G-d, and of other theological and philosophical concepts.

In Luria's view the creative process was not an uninterrupted sequence of causes and effects, nor a gradual descent of emanations. Creation is rather a process of "contractions" and "withdrawals," of "breakages" and "gaps," with intermittent gradual descents and regressions. This is how the doctrine of *tzimtzum* was cryptically formulated:

Know that before the emanations were emanated, and the creatures created, there was a simple supernal light filling up all reality, and there was no vacant space whatever....

And when it arose in His simple [i.e., uncaused] desire to create the worlds and to bring forth the emanated beings, in order to reveal the perfection of His acts, His Names, and His attributes, this being the reason for the creation of the worlds,....

The *En Sof* contracted (*tzimtzem*) Himself in the central point within Him, in the very center of His light, contracting that light, and withdrawing Himself towards the periphery around the central point, thus leaving a vacant place and sphere, and empty void, within the very center.

The nature of this *tzimtzum* is to reveal the root of judgment, in order subsequently to introduce the attribute of judgment into the worlds (for the attribute of *chesed* extends without limit, while that of judgment acts only by weight and measure).

After that *tzimtzum*, when there remained an "empty" space and vacant and empty sphere, within the center of the light of the *En Sof*, as stated above, a place was provided for the emanated, created, formed and made beings to exist therein. Thereupon He extended one straight line from His peripheral light downward toward the center of that space, the uppermost tip of which issuing from the *En Sof* itself and touching it...and in that space He caused all the worlds to be emanated, created, formed and made....[24]

---

24. R. Chaim Vital, *Etz Chaim*, at the beg; also his *Otzrot Chaim*, at the beg., and *Mevo She'arim*, chaps. 1 and 2.

The above formulation refers to the initial, or "great" *tzimtzum*, which was attended by a "breakage of the vessels" (*shevirat hakelim*), inasmuch as the Divine Light, contracted as it was, was still too profuse for the "vessels," causing them to shatter, scattering "sparks" (*nitzotzot*) throughout the primordial cosmic order, and thus again infinitely reducing the Divine light. The initial *tzimtzum* was followed by other *tzimtzumim*, in the process of which a cosmic order came into being, comprising the Four Worlds, to which reference will be made later on.

Luria's doctrine of *tzimtzum* and *shevirat hakelim* was shrouded in mystery and left room for ambiguity and anthropomorphisms. It was, however, more fully developed, refined and, in some respects, reinterpreted by Rabbi Schneur Zalman.

First of all, he eliminated any anthropomorphic notions which might have been, and have indeed been, inferred from the original formulation of the doctrine. Secondly, he expounded the doctrine by means of various illustrations which removed much of the mystery surrounding it, and made it more or less comprehensible to the less sophisticated mind. Finally, he made it the underlying basis of other related concepts in which Rabbi Schneur Zalman differs from his predecessors, notably, the concept of Divine Providence, the nature of evil, and others. It should be noted, however, that in the *Tanya* itself, with which we are concerned, the doctrine of *tzimtzum* is not treated at length, and is touched upon only insofar as it concerns the author's system of ethics. Consequently, our review of Rabbi Schneur Zalman's exposition of this doctrine will be made in somewhat broad outline, though we shall not limit ourselves to the *Tanya* and will draw upon the author's other works, as the occasion arises.

Tzimtzum is variously translated as "concentration," "contraction," "withdrawal," etc. Etymologically the word is derived from a root which is more closely related to "withdrawal," or "shrinkage." In this sense primarily Rabbi Schneur Zalman interprets this doctrine.

As the term applies to the doctrine of creation it means that the infinite power of the Creator is not limited to extension; it manifests itself just as well in *inextension* or *contraction*. In fact, it is in the power of *tzimtzum* that G-d's omnipotence is in greater

evidence than in extension. Were G-d's power limited to extension only, aside from the fact that that would not be compatible
with His attribute of omnipotence, there could never have come
into being *finite* existences, because all emanated beings would be
infinite, like Himself. Finite existences could therefore come into
being only by means of *tzimtzum*.

To say that G-d's infinite power manifests itself in contraction or inextension, sounds paradoxical; nevertheless this is what
creation postulates. Actually, if it is conceivable that G-d can
extend His attributes ad infinitum, it should be just as conceivable that G-d can contract His attributes *ad infinitum*.

The doctrine of *tzimtzum* will be more easily comprehended
by means of the illustrations used by Rabbi Schneur Zalman. A
teacher in expounding an idea to his pupil, his intellectual inferior, cannot present it in the terms of his own comprehension. He
must condense the idea, i.e., "reduce" it to the level of the pupil,
by means of illustrations and explanations comprehensible to the
pupil. Two aspects are here entailed: (a) that the pupil should
comprehend the idea, and (b) the condensed version must retain
all the elements of the original idea. Without such condensation,
the pupil will learn nothing, for in its original state the idea is
beyond the pupil's capacity of comprehension, and, moreover, if
it be forced upon him he will become so utterly confused as to
become incapable of grasping even subjects on his own level, his
mind ceasing to function properly.

When the upper, or teacher's, level is immeasurably higher
than the pupil's, when communication requires a radical descent,
it is necessary for the teacher to completely set aside the idea as
he conceives it, lest he fail to find terms accessible to the pupil.
Instead, he must start with a simpler idea, which is on an infinitely lower level than the original, and not directly related to it.
Subsequent amplifications will concern stages having a measura-
ble relationship with each other, which will eventually lead back
to a relationship with the original subject. In the latter instance
of the illustration the radical modification of the original idea
would be termed First, or Great, Condensation (*tzimtzum hari-
shon*, or *tzimtzum hagadol*). The ultimate purpose of the *tzimtzum*
process is to relate the upper level to the lower, on the part of the

teacher, while creating the capacity in the lower level to relate itself upwards to the higher level, on the part of the pupil.

Using the principle of *tzimtzum* as an explanation of creation, the process of creation is expounded something like this: Before the universe was created, there was only the *En Sof*, the Infinite, the One, the Absolute Unity, Whose Infinite Light filled all "space," including the space of the universe subsequently created. (The term "space" used here is not to be understood literally, since the very existence of space is a creation.) In the Infinite Light there was no "room" for finite existence. But the omnipotence of the Creator enabled Him to "withdraw" His Light into Himself, as it were, to create a "void" wherein finite existence could be created, by means of a tiny streak of light which was projected into this "void." This is the beginning of the process of *tzimtzum*, whereby the Infinite Light is so reduced abruptly and successively that finite beings can endure it.[25]

Elsewhere[26] the author explains this "withdrawal" of the Infinite Light within itself by means of a further analogy, from the working of the human mind. This analogy is designed to illustrate also that the act of withdrawal and extension involves no essential change in the agent. Suppose, says Rabbi Schneur Zalman, a person has fully and completely mastered a tractate of the Talmud, with all its commentaries, discussions, decisions, etc., all of which he knows fully and has "in his head." Should he then take up the study of another tractate and concentrate on it; or not concentrate on anything in particular, but simply rest his mind, what happens to the knowledge which he had acquired, but which he has temporarily dismissed from his mind? That knowledge, with all its details, is stored away somewhere in the recesses of his mind, for he can recall it at will, bring it out of its storage, review it, or hold a discourse on it. Thus, the human mind has the capacity for "expansion," i.e., expressing and manifesting itself in the form of "letters of thought"[27] (cogitation), as well as for "retraction," i.e., withdrawing itself back into its own shell, so to speak. In other words, the capacity of the mind to

25. *Tanya*, chaps. 21, 38, 48, 49.
26. *Likkutei Torah, Hosafot l'Vayikra*, pp. 51b ff., esp. 52 cf.
27. *Iggeret Hakodesh*, chap. 19, esp. p. 129a.

store knowledge and memories, and bring them out at will as the occasion demands, is simply the exercise of the mind in precluding the "light" of the intellect from manifesting itself constantly; otherwise all the stores of knowledge and experience which it had accumulated would tumble out together all at once in a chaotic jumble, without any intelligent results at all. Only by shutting off its infinite power, and permitting only a fraction of it to come forth, is intellectual activity made possible. That this process of expansion and retraction does not bring about any change in the essence of the mind is self-evident.

Analogy is not identity, and it is always necessary to make mental reservations when using this mode of inference, as Rabbi Schneur Zalman never tires of reminding us. Nevertheless, the working of the human mind, with its infinite capacity for producing an incessant flow of thoughts and its ability to combine extension with withdrawal (which, indeed, is the only manner of its normal functioning), provides a particularly apt illustration of the process of creation as conceived by Luria, and expounded by Rabbi Schneur Zalman.

In the process of creation, the infinite power of extension (the Infinite Light) was withdrawn, but it was not withdrawn completely. A "residue" (reshimu) was left which retained something of the pristine quality of the pre-tzimtzum light. This, together with the contracted ray of light that issued from it, combined to produce the "bifurcated" quality of a new post-tzimtzum light, in which the elements of infinitude and finitude are inherent, which produced a series of "lights" (orot) and "vessels" or "containers" (kelim), the former informing the latter; the latter "containing" the former. However, in the primordial phase of creation, the "lights" were too strong for the "vessels," resulting in the "Shattering of the Vessels" (shevirat hakelim), in the process of which the lights broke up into innumerable small "sparks" (nitzotzot) which scattered throughout the cosmic realm. On the principle that that which is highest falls lowest, the sublimest sparks became embedded in the lowest forms of material existence, and are in a state of "exile" in them, waiting to be "redeemed" through man's noble actions directly or indirectly relating to these objects.

The Great *Tzimtzum* was followed by other *tzimtzumim*, one succeeding the other in an innumerable series of "contractions," "screenings," and "condensations," in the process of which an infinite number of spiritual substances, or emanations, came into being, each "lower" than its predecessor in that it more effectively concealed the Light and Life flowing from the *En Sof*. Ours is the "lowest" world in the degree of the utmost concealment of the Infinite Light, where external matter completely conceals its true inner reality.[28]

The Cosmic Destiny

THE COSMIC ORDER WHICH came into being by means of the *tzimtzum* process comprises four main categories or levels, termed the Four Worlds: *Atzilut* ("Emanation"),[29] *Beriah* ("Creation"—a finite state radically different from its preceding World, *Atzilut*), *Yetzirah* ("Formation"—a lower state of finite existence), and *Asiyah* (literally "Action," or, "Making"),[30] the arche-type of our phenomenal world.

Each of these Four Worlds is an ordered universe of ten general categories, called *sefirot*, with innumerable subgradations which are described as "worlds" in themselves.

This unfolding process of creation extends from one extreme to the other, from the Light of the *En Sof*, which in its first emanation is coalesced with, and dissolved in, the *En Sof*, to "the other side" (*sitra achra*), the realm of the *kelipot*[31] ("shells" or

---

28. *Tanya*, chaps. 6, 24.
29. In Chabad the term *atzilut* is understood also in the sense of "proximity," from the Hebrew word *etzel*, "nearby."
30. The accepted translation of *Asiyah* by "World of Action" is neither descriptive nor definitive, for each of the Four Worlds constitutes Divine "action." The Four Worlds should be understood in terms of four developmental stages. We can best explain these terms by means of the following simple illustration. Suppose I conceive the idea of building a house. The materialization of the idea will pass through the following four stages: (1) the desire to have a house, as yet undefined; (2) a general mental idea of the house; (3) a detailed architectural design; (4) final construction. These four stages would generally correspond to the Four Worlds.
31. These terms are frequently found in the *Zohar* (e.g. I, 19b; II, 69b, 108b, 184; III, 185a, etc.) and are especially important in Lurianic Kabbalah.

"husks"), the forces of evil, wherein the "spark" that constitutes their true existence is so infinitely reduced as to be completely submerged and obscured by the outer shell.

The cosmic order of the unholy, or "other side," likewise comprises four main categories or levels, in an inverted order to the Four Worlds on the side of holiness. They are known as the four *kelipot*, of which the last three are called "completely unholy," while one is called the "translucent *kelipah*," which is predominantly unholy, but contains a measure of holiness. It is the transitional category between the holy and unholy side, and it is the spiritual counterpart of our physical world.[32]

Clearly, the unity of creation is upheld. The "other side" is not an independent realm; it is only the extreme end of the same creative process. Holiness and unholiness, or goodness and badness, essentially have the same substratum, like the two opposite poles of one magnet. The same creative force, the Light of the *En Sof*, that is responsible for the existence of the good and the holy is also responsible for the bad and the unholy, except that in the latter the Light of the *En Sof* has been reduced almost (but not quite) to the vanishing point. Being insensitive to the created force that keeps them in existence, the *kelipot*, or evil forces, are deluded, as it were, into thinking themselves independent and self-existent, defying the very hand that sustains them. Arrogance and humility are two basic characteristics of the unholy and holy, respectively, in their relationship to the *En Sof*. As for the relationship of the *En Sof* to them, the holy is said to be willed and desired; the unholy, merely tolerated. The holy receives its sustenance direct from the *En Sof*; the unholy is said to receive its sustenance "from behind the back,"[33] from the Divine "spark" that is in a state of "exile" in it.[34]

Having thus brought the whole of creation within one single hierarchy, which is unified by one single principle, the Light of the *En Sof*, the author has yet to explain how creation did not effect any change in the Creator. This is a matter of paramount importance to him not only as a philosophical truth, but as one

---

32. *Tanya*, chaps. 1, 4, 6, 22, 29, 37, etc.
33. Ibid., chap. 6; *Iggeret Hakodesh*, chap. 25.
34. Ibid., chaps. 17, 37, 39, 45.

that touches the very core of Jewish monotheism. Every Jew professes in his daily prayers, "Thou art He before the world was created, and Thou art He after the world was created."[35] "Thou" and "He" are the two aspects of the revealed and hidden G-d; of the same G-d Who is both revealed (Thou) and hidden (He). Creation, wherein the revealed aspect of the Light of the *En Sof* manifests itself, has not changed the Creator. How is this to be explained in simple terms so that every Jew could grasp it and not render mere lip service in professing his faith?

Here Rabbi Schneur Zalman draws upon a doctrine expounded by the Baal Shem Tov which is traceable to Luria and is based on the *Sefer Yetzirah*. It is the Kabbalistic doctrine of the Divine language as the substance of reality. According to this doctrine all things exist only by virtue of their participation in the Ten Fiats by which the world was created.[36] Quoting the Scriptures, "Forever, O Lord, Thy word endureth in the heavens,"[37] the Baal Shem Tov interpreted this passage as follows: G-d's word, declaring "Let there be a firmament,"[38] these very words and letters endure forever, constituting the very existence and reality of the heaven. Similarly, by an infinite number of letter configurations (*tzerufei otiot*), combinations and transmutations, all creatures came into being, the Hebrew letters of their name constituting the substance of their reality, the "soul" of everything, including the inanimate objects. These letter configurations are conceived as a form of *tzimtzum*, whereby the flow of creative force contained in the original Ten Fiats was contracted and fragmented into innumerable words and letters of reduced potency so as to enable them to inform the various created objects.[39] This whole doctrine is nothing but a particular aspect of the general theory of *tzimtzum* introduced by Luria, combined with the doctrine of the mystical power and the sacred alphabet and the 231 original configurations mentioned in *Sefer Yetzirah*.[40]

---

35. Liturgy, Morning Prayer.
36. *Avot* 5:1.
37. Psalms 119:89.
38. Genesis 1:6.
39. *Shaar Hayichud v'haEmunah* deals at length with this doctrine, as well as with those of Continuous Creation and Divine Providence.

We need not go into this doctrine at this point, though it is the basis of the Chasidic concept of Continuous Creation,[41] and its corollary that particular Divine Providence, contrary to Maimonides' view,[42] extends to every being, not only to man and to species.[43] What is important for us at this point is how Rabbi Schneur Zalman uses this mystical idea to explain in rational terms the immutability of G-d. Rabbi Schneur Zalman begins with a quotation of a familiar Biblical passage, namely, "By the word of G-d the heavens were made, and by the breath of His mouth all their hosts,"[44] and applies the analogy from the human word to illustrate his point. A syllable uttered by a person, says Rabbi Schneur Zalman, is quite insignificant in relation to the essential faculty of speech of the person, inasmuch as one has the capacity of uttering an endless stream of words. Even less significant is the word by comparison with the faculty of thought, where words originate. If we go a step further and consider the essence of the soul itself, what significance can an uttered word have by comparison with it? In a somewhat analogous manner the creation of the entire universe in its most com-

40. The number of 231 original configurations of the letters of the Hebrew alphabet is based on the mathematical formula $\frac{N(N-1)}{2}$, N being 22, the number of letters in the Hebrew alphabet. See also *Likkutei Amarim*, vol. II, tr. Nissen Mangel (Kehot, 1972), p. 14, n. 18.

41. The idea of *continuous creation* is not original with Chabad. It is already mentioned in ancient Hebrew liturgy, and recited daily in the Morning Prayer (in the Blessing of *Yotzer*): "In His goodness He renews each day, continuously, the work of Creation." (Comp. *Chagigah* 12b; cf. also Albo, *Ikkarim*, *Maamar* IV, ch. 8.) In Chabad, however, this doctrine receives an elaborate philosophical exposition, being fundamental to its whole system.

42. Cf. *Guide*, III, chaps. 17 and 18; also chap. 51. Nachmanides also shared this view. Cf. his commentary on Genesis 18:19. This seems to have been, in fact, the general view held by Jewish thinkers up to the time of the Baal Shem Tov, who introduced the new concept that Divine Providence extended to every particular not only in human beings, but also in the lower species, down to inanimate things.

43. The Baal Shem Tov taught that "even a leaf torn from a tree and swept by the wind from place to place reflects the Divine Will and Providence," *Likkutei Dibburim*, (Kehot, 1957-8), vol. I, p. 166. Cf. *Derech Chaim*, by Rabbi DovBer (son of Rabbi Schneur Zalman), *Shaar Hateshuvah*, chap. 9. *Iggeret Hakodesh*, chap. 25.

44. Psalms 33:6.

prehensive sense is but a "word" of G-d, and can no more affect the essence of the Creator as an uttered word can affect the essence of a human being. However, Rabbi Schneur Zalman hastens to qualify the analogy, whereby he gives the concept a deeper dimension. In the case of the human being, the word breathed out and uttered is something separate from him; in G-d, however, it cannot be anything separate, for there is nothing beside Him, and there can be no place devoid of Him; for He pervades and transcends everything; He is All, and everything remains within the All. Hence the analogy between the "word" of G-d and that of man would be closer if we conceive of the human word in its *potential* state, when it is still within the mind, before it was uttered, where it is in perfect unity with the intellect. In like manner, metaphorically speaking, the "word" of G-d and His thought, i.e., the created universe, are in perfect unity with His essence, even after they have been revealed in the form of creation, so that G-d remains the same before and after creation.[45]

However, the author of the *Tanya* continues, what has been said above is in relation to the Creator. In relation to the creatures there has, indeed, been a "change" in that they came into being. We who perceive everything by the senses, perceive corporeal things as separate and independent things. For, by virtue of G-d's infinite power to "contract" His Light to such a degree as to contain it within created and finite beings, these beings see themselves as separate creatures and consequently get the illusion that the Divine light and life (or the "word" of G-d) which is incorporated in them is also something separate from G-d.[46]

As the author states elsewhere:

Were the human eye permitted to see and perceive the life force that is in every created thing which is continuously flowing into it from the "utterance" and "breath" of G-d's mouth, none of its gross physical and material properties would appear to our eyes at all, for these would be nullified in the presence of the life-force preserving the thing, which is its true reality, since without this vitalizing

---

45. *Tanya*, chaps. 20, 21.
46. Ibid., end chap. 21.

and preserving force it would have no existence whatever, exactly as it was before Creation.[47]

If our world is the "lowest" and last in the chain of created worlds, below which there is no other, it follows, says Rabbi Schneur Zalman, that our material world is the ultimate object of creation. Moreover, all the upper worlds cannot have been created for their own sake, because their very existence involves only a regression (*yeridah*) from the Infinite Light. But the chain of the supernal worlds must have been created for the sake of this, our lowest world, where man was given the power to subjugate the forces of evil and turn darkness into light, a light which is all the brighter by virtue of the contrast with the darkness which it dispels. Thereby man makes it possible for G-d to have "an abode in the lowest world,"[48] and to derive "pleasure"[49] from the subjugation of the *sitra achra* and the conversion of darkness into light, a light which is superior to any light revealed in the upper worlds. It is in this "darkest" world that the process of regression can be reversed. Here the Infinite Light can blaze forth in a most intense way, illuminating not only this world but also the upper worlds.[50] For, to use another popular metaphor of Rabbi Schneur Zalman, by lifting up the foundation, the whole structure is lifted up.

The suppression of evil and illumination of the darkness of this world, will gradually lead to the complete sublimation of our physical world, a state of perfect holiness which it will reach in the Seventh Millennium.[51] It will be a state where nothing will any longer conceal the Infinite Light, and all evil will, as a matter of course, have been banished from the earth.

How is this "spiritualization" of the material world, which is its ultimate realization, to be accomplished?

---

47. *Shaar Hayichud v'haEmunah*, chap. 3.
48. *Tanchuma, Nasso* 16.
49. Cf. *Sifre, Shelach*, 15:17; *Pinchas*, 28:8.
50. *Tanya*, chap. 36.
51. Jewish tradition makes the present year (2007/8) the year 5768 (after Creation). Accordingly, we are approaching the end of the sixth millennium. The seventh ("Sabbatical") millennium is held to be the one that will see the fulfillment of Creation, ushered in by the Messianic Era and the Resurrection of the Dead. For his source the author makes reference to R. Isaac Luria's *Likkutei Torah*. Cf. *Tanya*, beg. chap. 37. Cf. also *Iggeret Hakodesh*, chaps. 4 and 26.

Our author has already referred to the cosmic implications of the performance of the Divine precepts, whereby man "repairs" the union of the creation with the Creator which has been disrupted, though only superficially, i.e., from the viewpoint of created beings, by the creation of matter. Developing this doctrine further, he postulates that every act of obedience to the Divine Will has a *lasting* and *cumulative* influence on the physical world, diminishing its evil and augmenting its good. And although the effect of each good act may not be immediately perceived, the cumulative effect will eventually manifest itself in the Messianic Era.

The author's confidence in the ultimate victory of the forces of light over those of darkness goes beyond commonplace optimism. It is bound up with his concept of the mystic order and the ultimate redemption of the world which, as he sees it, is inherent in creation itself. Creation was not intended to be justified only in the remote future. It offers an opportunity to man, indeed it is expected of him, that he utilize all his capacities to the end that creation should be justified *constantly*. In the future this will be *apparent* to all, but the process of fulfillment is going on even now; what is more, it is steady in its progress. Moral relapses in the world do not indicate flaws in this process; they are part of it and, if anything, are symptoms of the growing progress. The nearer the goal, the more critical is the struggle. It is to be expected, he maintains, that when the forces of light show strength, the opposing forces will endeavor to match it, and that the forces of evil should make their greatest "final stand" just on the verge of their total collapse.

CHAPTER III

ENDS AND MEANS

The Problem of Correlation and Interrelation

W e have now reached a point where we can proceed to examine Rabbi Schneur Zalman's basic concepts in a broader perspective. In doing so, we will have to fill in some gaps in order to round out his ethical system and bring it into final focus.

Rabbi Schneur Zalman conceives of man, universe and G-d in terms of internal unity, mutual relationship and overall correlation. On the individual level man must achieve inner harmony between his natural and his transcendental selves, recognizing the legitimate spheres of each. Such harmony man achieves by the sublimation of his earth-bound dispositions, whereby his physical body and animal soul becomes a vehicle for his real self, the transcendental Divine soul.

On the universal level, man is destined to bring about the supremacy of the forces of good over those of evil, leading to the eventual eradication of evil. This is his purpose in life.

Since man owes his life and existence to his Creator, he must justify himself in terms of the ultimate destiny of creation, and he must do so freely and of his own volition. Through correlating himself and the world in which he lives with the Creator, he becomes a partner in the creative effort which is of G-d. The over-all unifying principle lies, in the final analysis, in man's hands.

Rabbi Schneur Zalman's reflective thinking which starts with man leads him back to man. But here we are faced with a problem. The average individual—the *benoni*—is, according to Rabbi Schneur Zalman's own formulation, destined to spend his life in an endless inner conflict which is inherent in his two-dimensional nature. With constant vigilance and effort he can barely manage to keep the animal soul in check, so as to block it from taking possession, however temporarily, of any of the three "outer garments," namely, thought, speech and action. He is able to prevent his animal soul from expressing itself, but he cannot completely eradicate it, for such an accomplishment belongs to the "superior men" (*bnei aliyah*) who are few,[1] i.e., to the rare type of the *tzaddik*.

If such is the lot of the average man, it might well be asked, What is the purpose of this eternal human struggle? Besides, how could it be reconciled with the idea of a benevolent G-d? Would not the soul have been happier to remain in her celestial abode, basking in the light of the *En Sof* unhampered by physical garments, and free from conflicts?

Rabbi Schneur Zalman's answer is that human life on this earth (and by that is meant spiritual life, since the spirit is the true essence of the human being) is but a passing, albeit highly significant, phase in the life of the soul, which exists in a disembodied state both before and after its sojourn on this earth, and will again resume its terrestrial life after Resurrection.

The soul's descent into the physical body, which is only temporary, bestows a marked benefit on it. For although in its original state the soul adhered with undivided loyalty to its Creator, being a creature a gulf separated it from Him. Its descent into the lower world provides it with an opportunity to observe G-d's commandments which are the means of closing the gap between G-d and the soul. If the commandments are properly observed, the original gap will be lessened, and the soul will gain a higher degree of perception of the G-dhead. The soul's descent in effect becomes a means for its ascent.[2]

Moreover, it is also during its life on earth, embodied in the body and its animal soul, that the soul can span the gulf that sep-

1. *Sukkah* 45b; *Sanhedrin* 97b.
2. *Tanya*, chaps. 36-38.

arates it from its Creator and attain true unity with Him, the unity of essence with essence through the unity of will with will. Essence (*etzem*), as defined in Chabad, refers to the fundamental and absolute nature of a thing, considered independently of its manifestation. The essence and "quiddity" of G-d, as of the soul, cannot be known from their manifestation or existence. We have noted earlier[3] that the soul manifests itself through its soul-powers, which fall into two broad categories, which were termed General and Particular, respectively. Delight and Will belong to the former; the intellect and affections to the latter. To this must be added another distinction in that the Delight and Will are *essential* faculties, while the others are related or derivative. The Divine Will is an extension of the Divine Essence, as the soul's will is an extension of its essence. The Divine Will is embodied in the Divine Law. Therefore, by identifying its will to the Divine Will through the actual performance of the religious precepts, the soul attains the union of essence with essence which is of a higher order than the union that can be achieved intellectually while the soul is in its original state, before its descent into this world.

To attain this higher union, the Divine soul must overcome the natural dispositions of the animal soul which it informs. To this end, namely, the attainment of the supremacy of the spirit, man is committed by his very nature.

But while the soul's descent has an object connected with itself and is to this extent an end in itself, it has also an object outside of itself, for the attainment of which it is an agent. In other words, man has a two-fold destiny, a destiny which is related to himself personally and to the world he lives in.

Our material world, being the one that terminates the series of created world, is the end of creation. In this material world, man, according to the Biblical account, being the last of the creatures to be created, is the ultimate end of all creative acts. Contrary to Maimonides who holds that everything was created for its own sake and each thing has its own purpose,[4] Rabbi Schneur Zalman in company with all Kabbalists and some Jewish

---

3. See p. 24 f. above.
4. *Guide*, III, chaps. 13, 25.

philosophers,[5] insists that everything was created for the sake of man.[6]

But both man and the universe must be ordered to another and final end, which in itself is ordered to nothing further. That end, to Maimonides, is the will and wisdom of G-d. G-d's will and wisdom decreed the existence of the universe, and His wisdom created order, design and purpose in the universe. We cannot comprehend G-d's wisdom, hence we cannot know why His wisdom made the existence of the universe necessary, or why nonexistence should have preceded existence. However, because existence is undoubtedly good, G-d gave existence to all beings whose existence is possible.[7] The purpose of creation, according to Maimonides, is an internal one. To imply that the Creator has a purpose in creation outside of creation itself would imply a deficiency in the Creator and hence it is logically inadmissible.

Nevertheless, Rabbi Schneur Zalman pursues the problem further. Following the Kabbalists, Rabbi Schneur Zalman incorporates the concept of Delight as a third element in the creation of the universe.[8] "It pleased the Holy One, blessed be He, to have an abode in the lower worlds," they said;[9] "it delights G-d to see His will fulfilled,"[10] and "it pleases Him when the 'other side' (*sitra achra*) is subjugated and vanquished."[11] Delight, like will, is related to the essence and need have no external cause. However, in introducing the element of delight into the scheme of cre-

---

5. Notably R. Saadia Gaon, *Book of Beliefs and Opinions*, chap. 4, and R. Bachya ibn Pakuda, *Duties of the Heart*, chap. 2. A similar view was expressed by some Sages of the Talmud, e.g. *Brachot* 6b.

6. It should be noted that while R. Saadia Gaon shares this view, he arrives at it by rational categories. He sees man's superiority over all other creatures "in nothing else than in his being endowed with reason, with that Divine soul which, in the words of the Psalmist, makes him but 'a little less than G-d Himself.'" To Rabbi Schneur Zalman, however, the mystical aspect is more important, namely, the belief common to all Kabbalists that man is G-d's instrument through which the whole Creation attains fulfillment.

7. *Guide*, III, chap. 25.

8. The idea that G-d derives "pleasure" from His creatures is frequently found in the Bible. Cf. Psalms 104:31; 115:3; etc.

9. This frequently quoted passage is from *Tanchuma, Nasso*, 16.

10. *Sifre, Shelach* 15:7; *Pinchas* 28:8.

11. *Zohar*, III, 128a; f. at length.

ation, the Kabbalists placed man in a position of reciprocity with the Creator. The Kabbalists did not shrink from the idea that G-d needs man, or that man can please G-d, because they were not speaking of the unknowable, immutable, hidden G-d, but of G-d the Creator of the universe, in which man is the ultimate object of creation and the key to its fulfillment. In relation to this aspect of the Deity they saw nothing wrong in conceiving of a reciprocal interrelationship between the Creator and creation.

Rabbi Schneur Zalman applies this concept to good advantage in his system. The *benoni*, to be sure, is destined to experience the perennial conflict inherent in his two-dimensional nature. But, by Rabbi Schneur Zalman's definition, the *benoni* is in full control of the three "garments," namely, thought, speech and action. Every time he suppresses a sinful thought, or word, or natural disposition to commit an evil act, he "delights" his Maker and participates in the spiritualization of the universe.[12]

The Transcendency of the Divine Law

IN THE LIGHT OF THE PRECEDING DISCUSSION, the Divine precepts assume a new significance. G-d's will and delight are embodied equally in all the 613 precepts. Any attempt to differentiate between one precept and another on "rational" ground is basically illegitimate. At best, such a differentiation can have a bearing only on the external aspects of the Divine commandments. In Rabbi Schneur Zalman's view this would be a subjective and limited approach, for the fact that some precepts appear to us to be rational by virtue of their coincidence with our own concepts of morality, or utility, or the like, does not constitute their essential aspect. To him the essential quality of the Divine commandments must be sought in their intrinsic transcendency. Consequently, finite human reason can only grasp them partially, or approximately, but cannot fully comprehend them.

Thus, the subject of *taamei hamitzvot* (the reasons for the commandments)[13] presents an area where the mystical and

---

12. *Tanya*, chap. 27.

13. With very few exceptions, the commandments in the Torah are generally given as direct imperatives, without any reason or explanation why any partic-

rational approaches are conspicuous in their diversity. From the strictly rational point of view, it may be possible to find an explanation on purely rational grounds for all, or almost all, of the 613 precepts, as Maimonides has demonstrated in his *Guide*. Moreover, if, as he states, "the knowledge of G-d is the only source of eternal life,"[14] it becomes imperative to find a rational explanation for those commandments, the didactic value of which is not plainly in evidence. Indeed, Maimonides sees himself impelled to uncover the rational basis of the so-called "suprarational" commandments.

Rabbi Schneur Zalman will readily agree that all the Divine commandments have, undoubtedly and as a matter of course, important didactic value and are also useful in many other respects. However, he is not concerned with these "external" aspects. He insists that the ultimate and essential value of the commandments lies in their being the vehicle of attachment to G-d, whereby finite man transcends his finitude and partakes of the Infinite. Hence, the primary condition of attaining this attachment is not knowledge, which is necessarily limited, but unlimited obedience and submission to the will of G-d, in whatever commandment G-d's will is expressed, and regardless of its degree of rationality as measured by our understanding.

This does not mean that Rabbi Schneur Zalman is anti-intellectual. Far from it. He rejects the idea that blind faith is all that is required in man's relationship to G-d. Indeed, as we have seen,[15] his insistence on intellectual comprehension was regarded by some of his colleagues as a "deviation" from the Beshtian emphasis on faith. With R. Bachya ibn Pakuda, Rabbi Schneur Zalman holds that "knowledgeable performance is superior to blind obedience."[16] But to Rabbi Schneur Zalman it is superior

---

ular precept should be observed. This has given rise to a vast body of literature, where attempts have been made to find various explanations, or reasons, for particular precepts on moral, ethical, social, or other didactic grounds. In Chabad, the emphasis is on the mystical nature of the Divine commandments as the vehicle for attachment to G-d, with *kedushah* (holiness) as the essential substratum of all the commandments. See Mindel, *The Commandments*. The subject will be further discussed in the next volume.

14. *Guide*, III, chap. 27.

15. See Mindel, *Rabbi Schneur Zalman of Liadi*, Vol. 1, p. 189 ff.

16. Duties of the Heart, 3:3.

not because knowledge *per se* necessarily adds to the quality of attachment, but rather because such performance means obedience plus knowledge, that is to say, because in such performance the human intelligence also, and not only the human will, participates; in other words, the *whole* man is then engaged in the Divine service.

Subjectively speaking, i.e., from the point of view of individual performance, there can, of course, be differences in the degree of attachment to G-d attained by one individual as compared to another, or in the performance of one commandment as compared to another in the same individual. However, insofar as the Divine commandments themselves are concerned, there can be no distinction in their intrinsic quality: all are the will and wisdom of G-d, and in the fulfillment of one as of the other man identifies himself with the will of G-d and partakes of the same source and degree of holiness. This, incidentally, is also the view of Maimonides in his Code,[17] where the philosophic aspect is less evident. But even in the *Guide*, especially in its concluding chapters, Maimonides appears to emphasize the mystical aspect of the commandments in terms of communication with G-d. Certain passages from that section of the *Guide* could fit very harmoniously into the *Tanya*. By way of illustration we may well quote the following passage:

> Note.—I have shown you that the intellect which emanates from G-d unto us is the link that joins us to G-d. You have it in your power to strengthen that bond, if you choose to do so, or to weaken it gradually till it breaks, if you prefer this. It will only become strong when you employ it in the love of G-d, and seek that love; it will be weakened when you direct your thoughts to other things. You must know that even if you were the wisest man in respect to the true knowledge of G-d, you break the bond between you and G-d whenever you turn your thoughts entirely to the necessary food or any necessary business; you are then not with G-d, and He is not with you; for that relation between you and Him is actually interrupted in those moments....

---

17. *Hilchot Me'ilah* 8:8.

> We must bear in mind that all such religious acts as reading the Law, praying, and the performance of other precepts, *serve exclusively as the means of causing us to occupy and fill our mind with the precepts of G-d*, and free it from worldly business; for we are thus, as it were, in *communication with G-d*, and undisturbed by any other thing.[18]

If one be permitted at all to make any distinction between the "rational" precepts and the "supra-rational" (the *chukkim*), the latter would, in Rabbi Schneur Zalman's view, assume a more significant importance for the worshipper, precisely because of their "supra-rational" character. In the performance of the moral acts, the worshipper may unconsciously introduce a personal element, his own rationality or natural disposition. One may, for example, act morally by the dictates of one's own reason, which would detract from their holiness; or one may act benevolently purely out of the goodness of one's heart, or because one cannot bear to see others suffer, or because one may expect something in return, or out of any other natural disposition. Nothing of this sort can mar a purely religious act which is motivated by a desire for holiness and communion with G-d. It is interesting to note that Halevi, too, attached greater significance to the *chukkim*, but for another reason. The moral and ethical precepts were more or less common to all religions; the *chukkim* were peculiarly Jewish and related to the "Divine influence" and the chosenness of the Jewish people.[19]

Although all the Divine precepts are essentially the same, Rabbi Schneur Zalman takes note of the distinction accorded by the Rabbis to certain precepts, notably the study of the Torah[20] and the practice of *tzedakah* ("acts of benevolence").[21] He explains the excellence of these two precepts in terms of apprehension of the Infinite.

The Torah embodies the wisdom of G-d. When a person is engaged in the study of the Torah, there is an intellectual communion between the human intellect and the Divine Intellect,

---

18. *Guide*, tr. Friedlander, p. 386. Italics added.
19. *Kuzari* II, 48.
20. *Peah* 1:1.
21. *Bava Batra* 10a f.

and since wisdom is the first faculty, and of all faculties the closest to the essence of the soul, intellectual communion leads to
essential communion, namely, the unity of essence with essence.
Moreover, when the human intellect is engaged in the study of
the Torah and apprehends its wisdom to the utmost extent of its
capacity, it is not only absorbed in the Divine Wisdom, but the
latter is, at the same time and to that extent, absorbed in the
human intelligence. There is thus attained a reciprocal and inter-
locking union between the finite and the Infinite, where all bar-
riers are dissolved in the merging of the two. Such a perfect
union, Rabbi Schneur Zalman emphasizes, is possible only
through the comprehension of the Torah, surpassing in quality
even the union attained by the performance of the precepts; for
the latter involve primarily the "outer garments," namely, speech
and action, while the former involves the "inner garment" of
thought. Hence, in the case of the ritual, the Infinite Light is said
to merely "encompass" the soul, as it were, without thoroughly
pervading it, as it does in the case of the study and comprehension of the Torah, when it touches the essence of the soul.
Symbolically, the precepts are said to provide the "garments" of
the soul, while the study of the Torah provides both a "garment"
and a "food." This explains, says Rabbi Schneur Zalman, the
Rabbinic statement that "the study of the Torah balances against
all other commandments combined."[22]

Parenthetically it may here be added that, as can be seen
from the above, whatever justification there may be in the alle-
gation that the study of the Torah has been subordinated to the
ritual in Chasidut, it cannot be included in the tenets of the
Chabad system. Nowhere else as in the *Tanya* and in Chabad literature in general do we find such emphasis on the significance
of the study of the Torah and Talmud, including such sections
and minutiae therein which are entirely abstract, hypothetical
and apparently irrelevant to the daily life.[23]

On the other hand, Rabbi Schneur Zalman points out that
the performance of the ritual is invested with mystical aspects
which, in certain respects, surpass even the excellence of intel-

22. *Peah* 1:1. *Tanya*, chaps. 4, 5, 23, 37, etc.
23. *Tanya*, chaps. 1, 5, 8, 23, etc.

lectual activity. For, while the Torah embodies the Wisdom of G-d, the precepts constitute the Will of G-d, and, as has been observed, the Will is even more closely related to essence than the faculty of Wisdom. Of course, where the study of the Torah is undertaken also as a Divine commandment, i.e., as the Divine Will, its excellence among the Divine precepts will be second to none. There will remain, nevertheless, this important distinction. The performance of the ritual, involving as it does physical action and, in most cases, also some physical object, contributes, in a direct and immediate way, to the sublimation and spiritualization of the animal soul and physical body, as well as of Nature in general.[24]

Furthermore, where the ritual is performed not mechanically, but with real intention (*kavanah*), it involves all three of the "garments," thought, speech and action, and in that case embraces the whole of man in his communion and attachment to the Divine Being. Hence, the practical precepts have an advantage over the study of the Torah, where only one, or at best two, of the "garments" are involved, namely, those of thought and speech. This consideration is significant for the all-important doctrine of *tikkun* mentioned in our earlier discussions.[25] It is connected, more specifically, with the soul's mission in its descent into the physical world, since the Divine soul is pure and sinless, and requires no *tikkun* for itself.[26]

The above discussion is particularly relevant to the commandment of *tzedakah*, concerning which the Rabbis also said that it balances against all other precepts combined. This statement seems incompatible with the statement that the study of the Torah equals all other precepts combined, for, at first glance, both statements cannot be logically true. In Halachah, the two statements are reconciled by a modification of the statement about *tzedakah*, An act of benevolence has precedence over Torah study only when it is one that cannot be postponed, or performed by others. Hence the Halachic ruling is that the study of the Torah should not be interrupted for the performance of those

---

24. Ibid., chap. 35.
25. See pp. 50f. above.
26. *Tanya*, chap. 37.

good deeds which can be done by others; otherwise, the latter take precedence.[27] In the light of our author's interpretation, however, the contradiction is resolved more subtly. In terms of communion with G-d, declares Rabbi Schneur Zalman, the study of the Torah is supreme; in terms of *tikkun*, i.e., spiritualizing the physical body and environment, the precept of *tzedakah* takes first place, inasmuch as it represents a "total effort." For, when a person gives away to the poor some of the money he earned through the effort of his body and mind, he gives away more of himself than in the performance of any other precept.[28] For this reason, the author points out, the precept of *tzedakah* is throughout the Palestinian Talmud referred to as *The Precept*, and the Rabbis also said that *tzedakah* hastens the arrival of the Messianic era.[29] For, as has been said earlier, this era is contingent upon the full "spiritualization" of the physical world. Thus, once again, the purity of intention assumes a crucial importance. *Tzedakah*, like all other precepts, must be practised purely as a Divine commandment, unmarred by any other consideration.[30]

Kavanah in Prayer and Performance

THE SUBJECT OF KAVANAH (the intention or thought that must accompany every religious act), which we must now take up, has often been misunderstood in relation to its significance in earlier Kabbalah, in Lurianic Kabbalah, and in Chasidut.

It would take us too far afield to examine the various misconceptions associated with the doctrine of *kavanah*. It is certain, however, that in the *Tanya kavanah*, on its higher level, is conceived in terms of *devekut*.[31] This is all the more significant in view of the fact that Rabbi Schneur Zalman adopted the Lurianic ritual of prayer with its attending *kavanot*.[32]

---

27. Ibid.; *Mo'ed Katan* 9b; *Tur Shulchan Aruch*, par. 246, 18.

28. *Tanya*, chap. 37.

29. *Bava Batra* 10a; *Shabbat* 138a.

30. Actually the Rabbis permitted latitude of personal motivation in the case of *tzedakah*, since the poor and needy must be helped regardless. Cf. e.g. *Pesachim* 8a; *Rosh Hashanah* 4a; *Bava Batra* 15b.

31. *Tanya*, chap. 38. *Kuntres haAvodah*, by Rabbi Sholom DovBer Schneersohn, (Kehot, 1946), in the beg.

Kavanah in the sense of *devekut*, that is to say, the intention to attain unity with G-d, is, of course, not confined to prayer; it applies equally to all religious precepts. In prayer, however, the question of *kavanah* is of greater concern inasmuch as prayer is largely meditative. Hence, it has been said, "Prayer without *kavanah* is like a body without a *neshamah* (soul)."[33] In view of the special importance attached to prayer in the Chasidic thought in general, and in Chabad in particular, it will be well to acquaint ourselves with what Rabbi Schneur Zalman has to say on this subject in the *Tanya* and elsewhere.

Rabbi Schneur Zalman's concept of prayer is based on the Baal Shem Tov's teachings which introduced a radical change of attitude toward this institution in Jewish life.

The learned and scholarly class of Jews had inherited a somewhat condescending attitude towards prayer.[34] To a considerable extent this attitude had to do with a natural disposition. The Talmudist, for whom the wisdom of the Divine Law was like an endless ocean, where new continents were ever to be discovered, the daily recitation of prayer, which follows a fixed pattern and text, did not seem to offer much intellectual stimulus or gratification. The prayers are fairly simple, even for unlearned Jews, and the very familiarity with them tends to detract from their inspiring quality. In the daily repetition of the community liturgy there seems no room for individuality, originality, self-assertion, or any intellectual advancement. Small wonder that community prayer had deteriorated to a form of habitual performance. The scholar could only reluctantly and with resignation tear himself away

---

32. Rabbi Schneur Zalman's Siddur (—"According to the Lurianic ritual") was first published in Shklov, 1803. Cf. also Aaron Wertheim, *Halachot V'halichot Bachasidut* (Jerusalem, 1960), pp. 94-96 and 100-143.

33. Cf. *Shnei Luchot Habrit*, vol. I, p. 249b. *Tanya*, chap. 38.

34. This despite the importance attached to prayer in the Talmud and Halachah. Maimonides, in the *Code* (beg. of *Hilchot Tefillah*), rules that daily prayer is a positive commandment of the Torah (not merely a Rabbinic enactment). On the other hand, prayer seems to have been subordinated to the study of the Torah. Cf, e.g., *Rosh Hashanah* 35a; *Yerushalmi, Brachot* 7a (no less an authority than Rabbi Shimon ben Yochai); *Shabbat* 10a; etc. However, this is not the place for a lengthy discussion, especially as the subject has been amply treated by others.

from his absorbing studies to recite the prayers together with the laity. If he recited the prayers quickly, with a touch of impatience perhaps, it was understandable. But it was inevitable, at the same time, that such an attitude to prayer on the part of the scholar and Talmudist should minimize its importance in the eyes of the community as a whole. Prayer often became like a formality which had to be gotten over as quickly as possible. Only on certain occasions, notably during the High Holidays, did prayer assume greater importance.

One of the basic objectives of the Baal Shem Tov was to redeem the congregational service and place it in the very center of Jewish religious life. He taught that in the very simplicity of the liturgy, in its precluding all forms of originality and self-assertion, lies its very significance as the true vehicle of communion with G-d. It is through prayer that the worshipper can cultivate a sincere feeling of attachment to the *En Sof*, and it is in prayer that a person can attain true humility, selflessness and purity of heart. For in the performance of other acts of Divine worship, there is a greater possibility of some ulterior motive creeping in, consciously or unconsciously, to mar the purity and holiness of the act. In study, for instance, there is the gratification derived from comprehension and the sense of personal accomplishment; in the performance of good works there may creep in some selfish motive. Prayer, however, is strictly a matter of communion between the worshipper and his Maker. It is in this sense that Rabbi Schneur Zalman conceives of the essential quality of prayer, as he inherited it from his master, and for this reason it occupies a pivotal place in his system.

Tefillah, which is generally rendered as "prayer," has little to do with any such connotation as "begging," or "requesting," which "prayer" literally means. Surely, it cannot be the purpose of prayer to appeal to G-d for His benevolence, for "it is in the nature of the good to do good" without request; no child has to appeal to its father for the elementary necessities of life. Nor can it be said that G-d needs to be reminded of our needs.

To be sure, there is the commandment to "cry" to G-d in times of trouble,[35] but the purpose of such supplication, as

---

35. Numbers 10:9.

Maimonides reminds us,[36] is to establish the principle that we recognize G-d as the master of the world, Who can help us in our
hour of need. By turning to Him in times of trouble, or triumph,
we cultivate our faith in G-d's providence; we reaffirm our belief
that He takes notice of each and every one of us, and of our ways
and actions, and that He can make them succeed or fail. In the
light of this, regular daily prayer serves to remind us continually
of G-d, and of our duty to fear Him and love Him, and to keep all
His commands.

To this Rabbi Schneur Zalman adds several profound insights
and concepts.[37]

On the basis of the *Zohar*,[38] which sees in Jacob's dream of the
ladder which "stood on earth, its top reaching into the heaven,"[39]
an allusion to prayer, linking man with G-d, Rabbi Schneur
Zalman develops the concept of prayer in terms of "rungs" or
stages, one higher than the other, elevating man to the highest
level of union with G-d.

The basic aspect of prayer as formulated by Maimonides
above, is but the first rung. The meaningful words of the daily
prayers, the good resolutions which prayer brings forth, are transformed into angels which go up to G-d, and G-d sends down
angels with blessings in return. That is why Jacob saw in his
dream that the angels were "going up and coming down,"
although one would have expected angels to come down first and
then to go up.

On a higher level, the Hebrew word *tefillah* is seen in its
derivative meaning from the word *pallel*, to "judge," i.e., make a
distinction between good and bad, or execute judgment.[40] The
reflexive verb *hitpalel*, to pray or intercede, thus also means "to
judge oneself." In this sense, Rabbi Schneur Zalman considers
prayer as the time of self-judgment and self-evaluation. When a
person addresses himself to G-d and prays for His blessings, he

---

36. *Guide*, III, chaps. 36, 44.
37. See Mindel, *As For Me—My Prayer*, Introduction (Kehot, 1972).
38. *Zohar* I, 149b. *Torah Or*, 88a; *Likkutei Torah*, Beshalach 2b. Cf. also R.
Schneur Zalman's Introduction to his Siddur, vol. I.
39. Genesis 28:12.
40. E.g. I Samuel 2:25; Ezekiel 16:52; Psalms 106:30. As a noun (פלילים) Judges,
occ. Exodus 21:22; Deuteronomy 32:31.

must inevitably search his heart and examine himself whether he measures up to the standards of daily conduct which G-d had prescribed for man to follow. If he is not one who fools himself, he will be filled with humility, realizing that he hardly merits the blessings and favors for which he is praying. This is why our prayers stress G-d's infinite goodness and mercies, praying to G-d to grant our requests not because of our merits, but even though we do not deserve it. For this reason, also, our prayers, on weekdays, contain a confession of sins which we may have committed knowingly or unknowingly. We pray for G-d's forgiveness and resolve to better ourselves, by living up more fully to the way of the Torah and *mitzvot* which G-d commanded us.

On a still higher level, prayer becomes *avodah*, "service," as already defined by the Sages with reference to the Biblical commandment, "To serve Him with all your heart"[41]—"What is heart-service? Service of the heart is Prayer."[42] Rabbi Schneur Zalman elaborates: The plain meaning of *avodah* is "work," "hard labor." We work with a raw, sometimes coarse, material until it is converted into a refined, finished product. In the process, the coarseness and impurities of the raw material are removed. The tanner, for example, takes raw hide and by various processes converts it into fine leather. The parchment on which a Torah scroll is written, or a Mezuzah, or Tefillin, is made of the hide of a kosher animal.

Moral refinement likewise entails hard work. It is no small effort to overcome such traits as pride, anger, and the like, which stem from the animal soul in man, but prayer is the "refinery," where the impurities of character are done away with. During prayer, our Divine soul speaks to G-d, and even the animal soul is then filled with holiness. We feel cleansed and purified by such "service," and, if it is truly heart-service and not lip-service, the feeling of purity and holiness lingers on and raises the daily conduct to the level of holiness expected of the "kingdom of priests and holy nation."[43]

The highest rung on the "ladder" of prayer is reached when

---

41. Deuteronomy 11:13.
42. *Sifri*; *Taanit* 2a.
43. Exodus 19:6.

we are so inspired as to want nothing but attachment with G-d. On this level, *tefillah* means "union," having an etymological connection with the verb *niftalti*.[44] It is also related to the verb (occurs in Mishnaic Hebrew) *tofel*, to attach, or join, or bind together, as two pieces of an earthen vessel are cemented together to make it whole again.[45]

The Divine soul, which is a "part of G-dliness indeed," longs to be reunited with, and absorbed in, G-dliness; just as a small flame, when it is brought close to a larger flame, tends to be absorbed into the larger flame. The soul has in fact been called the "candle of G-d."[46] The flame of a candle is restless, striving upwards, as if to break away from the wick and body of the candle; for such is the nature of fire—to strive upwards. The soul, too, strives upwards, like the flame of a candle. Such is its nature, whether one is conscious of it or not. This, incidentally, also explains why a Jew naturally sways while praying. For the time of prayer is the most propitious occasion for attachment of "spirit to spirit," and in doing so, the soul, as it were, flutters and strains upwards, to be united with G-d.[47]

Thus, on the highest level, as conceived by Rabbi Schneur Zalman, the worldly needs of the worshipper are totally disregarded in prayer, and all references to life, health, prosperity and the like are understood in a spiritual sense only: "life" is then understood as the experience of communion with the Living G-d; "health"—the wholesomeness and harmony of the inner self; "prosperity," "riches," "blessings"—all are understood in terms of the *real* and eternal good that comes from closeness with the *En Sof*, For this reason, Rabbi Schneur Zalman points out, the daily prayers have been permanently arranged in such a way as to lead up, step by step, in a crescendo of outpouring of the heart and the effusion of the yearning soul seeking to reach the height of communion. As mentioned earlier, prayer is the symbolic Jacob's ladder, "standing upon the earth with its top reaching into heaven."

---

44. Genesis 30:8. See Rashi ad loc., quoting Menachem ibn Saruk; so also *Rashbam. Ibn Ezra* interprets it in the sense of intwisted, "as in wrestling."
45. *Tosfot, Pesachim* 5:9.
46. Proverbs 20:27.
47. *Tanya*, chaps. 19, 46.

On the "ladder" of prayer the worshipper rises from personal grat-itude to G-d for His benevolence, to the free effusion of the heart. The daily prayers are introduced through the moving psalms of praise, extolling the majesty and holiness of the Creator; thence they proceed to the affirmation of the unity of G-d in "Hear, O Israel, the Lord is our G-d, the Lord is One,"[48] where *our* G-d, the G-d of our experience is the One and All, the transcending *En Sof*. This is the prelude to our complete identi-fication with Him through profound love, transcending our very existence, as we become conscious of "And thou shalt love the Lord thy G-d with all thy heart, and with all thy soul, and with all thy might."[49]

Elsewhere[50] the author interprets the tradition[51] that the three daily prayers were originally instituted by the three Patriarchs, Abraham, Isaac and Jacob, in the light of the Kabbalah, according to which the three Patriarchs were the embodiment of the three qualities of love, fear and mercy, respec-tively. The prayers are thus imbued with the mystic attribute of being able to evoke the said innate qualities of the Divine soul, namely, fear and love of G-d, as well as a sense of pity for its being in "bondage," under the influence and distraction of the animal soul. Through prayer, these innate, though sometimes obscured, higher emotions are given free play, until they are diffused throughout one's inner being, including the animal soul. The Divine soul is thus "released," its shackles are broken, and it sprouts wings to soar heavenward.[52]

The "deliverance" of the soul during, and by means of, prayer is allegorically identified with the great historic event of the Exodus from Egypt. "Enslavement and liberation" become a daily experience. "Liberation from Egypt" is not merely an event of the dim past; it must be achieved in daily life. "Egypt"—in Hebrew,

---

48. Deuteronomy 6:4.
49. Ibid., 6:5. Cf. *Likkutei Torah, Nasso*, p. 26b; *Tavo*, p. 42d; *Shir Hashirim*, p. 43b.
50. *Likkutei Torah, Emor*, p. 35c.
51. *Brachot* 26b.
52. This concept of the "deliverance" of the soul is, obviously, radically differ-ent from the concept of the soul being a "prisoner" of the body which sees its deliverance in the mortification of the flesh.

Mitzraim, which through a change of vowels yields *metzarim*, or "limitations"—is symbolic of the distressing obstacles and limitations imposed on the Divine soul by the material aspects of life connected with the body and the natural soul. These must be overcome. For while the Divine soul is "sentenced" to life-long confinement in the clay frame of a body which it shares with a domineering animal soul, this is not a punishment which it has to endure with resignation. On the contrary, the soul is pure and guiltless, but it has a mission to accomplish. Like the children of Israel who were to depart "with great treasure,"[53] as it is esoterically explained, the soul is sent down to this earth to acquire treasures which it cannot acquire while in its pristine state—all the treasures connected with *acts* and performances of the pious deeds on this earth, a mission which, as has been noted, is connected with the purification and spiritualization of the gross material world as a whole, "elevating" the soul's share of the entire Creation to its ultimate fulfillment in the unity of the Creator.

Therefore the "prisoner" is not placed at the mercy of the prison-warden, the animal soul, to languish in its dark cell; such an idea is incompatible with the mercy and goodness of the Creator. Nay, the "prisoner" is given the key to open his cell doors and leave his prison at least three times a day. Born in prison, the prisoner may not be aware of the green pastures, warm sunshine and bright light that awaits him outside the prison walls. Indeed, some prisoners, who have never used their keys to freedom, remain entombed, never seeing the light. But he who uses the key and tastes the light and warmth of a free life, will want to repeat the experience regularly. He may be so enthralled, indeed, as to be loath to return to his cell. He will, moreover, take the "prison-warden" with him and let him share, and thus double, the joy.

Such is our author's conception of prayer as allegorically exemplified in the "Exodus from Egypt."[54] It is the key to communion with G-d, that feeling of oneness with the Infinite which is experienced when the Infinite Light floods the soul, embracing

53. Genesis 15:16.
54. *Tanya*, chaps. 31, 47.

and pervading it completely. And this experience is to be found in prayer more than in any other form of worship or pious acts because, for one thing, the experience of prayer lends itself to greater humility and self-effacement; and for another, because prayer is more meditative. In a similar way *kavanah* is important, though not quite to the same extent, in the performance of every religious act.

The question of *kavanah* does not, of course, originate in Kabbalah. It first received attention in the Talmud, as a question in Halachah. Our author proceeds from this point, and as on other occasions when the Halachah and the Kabbalah cross paths in our author's thought, the result is not a clash but a synthesis.

The Halachist is, first and foremost, interested in the legal aspect of *kavanah*, i.e., to what extent, if any, specific intention is a necessary prerequisite of a religious act. It is generally recognized that in most cases of purely religious acts, no special intention is required, since the act itself is evidence of the intention to perform the particular religious duty. Nor is there any difference of opinion in regard to such cases where intention is clearly lacking, in which case the act itself does not constitute performance of the religious duty. Such is the case, for instance, when a person blows the *shofar* on Rosh Hashanah for practice, and he would be required to blow the Shofar again with the intention to fulfill the religious duty. On the other hand, there may be instances where the presence of intention is in doubt, and it is in such instances that Rabbinic opinion may be divided as to whether or not 'the religious obligation was fulfilled. At any rate, in Halachah the primary concern with *kavanah* is in terms of "intention," i.e., in the sense of performing a precept "for its own sake," or "for the sake of heaven," when it is in a true sense an act of obedience to the Divine commandment. *Kavanah* in the sense of "devotion," that is in terms of "quality" of the act, is of secondary consideration, except in certain areas where quality is of the essence, such as in the study of the Torah, or in the practice of charitable acts, and the like. In relation to these acts the Rabbis have enunciated the principle that "It matters not whether one does much or little, so long as one's heart is directed to heaven,"[55] or "The Holy One, blessed be He, desires the heart."[56]

In Kabbalah, especially in Lurianic Kabbalah, a new dimension was added to *kavanah*. For inasmuch as the Divine commandments were conceived in terms of mystical communion with G-d, the attunement of heart and mind becomes essential. In Lurianic thought, the mystical content of *kavanah* was further deepened by the doctrines of *tzimtzum* and of the "Breaking of the Vessels." The performance of the Divine commandments brings about the "redemption of the Divine sparks" which had been scattered throughout the created worlds since the primordial "Breaking of the Vessels." Thus a still further dimension was added to *kavanah* in terms of *yichud* and *tikkun*—the reunification and restoration of the original Divine Unity which, to all appearance, had been disturbed in the process of creation.

Rabbi Schneur Zalman integrated elements of all these concepts of *kavanah* and poured them into mystico-rational vessels of his own system, as will become discernible in our further discussion of the subject.

Our author introduces the subject of *kavanah*[57] with a reference to the Halachah, which rules that meditation cannot take the place of speech, so that if one "reads" the *Shema* merely in his thoughts, even with the fullest force of his *kavanah*, he does not fulfill the requirement of the law. Similarly in regard to Grace after the meal and other benedictions. However, if he utters the words with his lips without inner *kavanah*, he generally fulfills the requirement of the law *ex post facto*, except in the case of the first verse of *Shema* and the first benediction of the *Amidah*.[58]

It would seem from the above ruling that in all cases except the two instances involved, the word rather than the thought is of the essence. However, as our author sees it, the articulation of words is required because a *physical* effort is demanded in the performance of a pious act, as our author has so often emphasized, in order to achieve *tikkun*. This is based on the premise that the Divine soul itself is essentially pure and that its task during its life on this earth is to illuminate the physical body and animal soul

---

55. *Brachot* 17a.
56. *Sanhedrin* 106b.
57. *Tanya*, chap. 38.
58. *Brachot* 13b.

with the light of the *En Sof*, which cannot be accomplished by meditation alone, since that is an exercise of the mind and not of the body.

Nevertheless, physical performance without meditation on the deeper aspects of the act, deprives the worshipper of the profound religious experience inherent in the act, and at the same time achieves only a partial diffusion of the light of the *En Sof*. Where the worshipper is capable of intelligent meditation which evokes the highest order of fear and love of G-d, attended by the utmost effusion of the soul and a thirst for *devekut*, which permeates his performance of the commandment or his study and prayer, such *kavanah* is of a higher order, corresponding to the "soul" that animates a human being. On the other hand, the worshipper whose capacity for meditation is limited to his inherent *natural* love and fear of G-d, whereby his animal soul participates only passively in the conscious desire of the Divine soul to attain *devekut* through the performance of the precepts and prayer—his *kavanah* is of a lower order, corresponding to the "soul" of the dumb animals whose actions are animated by their instincts, rather than by intelligence and freedom as in the case of man.[59]

As might be expected, the higher form of *kavanah* is to be found in the Divine service of the *tzaddik*. It is said to diffuse the Infinite Light with such intensity as to reach the highest of the four spiritual worlds, the World of Emanation. While the lower form of *kavanah* is that of the *benoni*, which is said to reach only the lower spiritual worlds of Creation, Formation and Action. However, where prayer, or the actual performance of a commandment, is done without *any kavanah*, but simply as a matter of habit and thoughtless formality, such service accomplishes nothing in the diffusion of the Infinite Light, and, lacking the intention for *devekut*, remains in a state of separateness, "floating" as it were, in a world of its own, until such time as it is taken upward by meditative prayer and pious acts. In other words, though the absence of *kavanah* clips the wings of prayer or pious acts, they are, nevertheless, potentially good.

In this connection we are treated to a reinterpretation of the

---

59. *Tanya*, chap. 38. Cf. *Shnei Luchot Habrit*, vol. I, p. 249b, where two categories of *kavanah*, "esoteric" and "exoteric," are distinguished.

Rabbinic concept of *lishmah*, "for its own sake," as it applies to religious acts. In our author's view, a habitual performance of a religious act which one has been trained to perform from one's earliest youth cannot, in a human being, be quite devoid of some attending thought or awareness. It is difficult, our author states, to imagine a human being daily performing religious acts in complete absentmindedness. Some degree of fear or love of G-d is necessarily involved, but because it is so unimaginative, it lacks the strength of full-fledged "wings" to soar upward. On the other hand, should the performance of the religious act be tainted by some personal or selfish motive, however harmless, then it descends into "exile" in the *kelipat nogah* and is held there until it is "released" by repentance. It is only this form of "innocent" ulterior motive (such as studying the Torah in order to become a recognized scholar) that the Rabbis condoned, and even encouraged, by stating, "Let a man engage in the Torah and precepts even not for their own sake, since he will eventually attain thereby performance for its own sake."[60] For, sooner or later, he will repent and redeem his actions.[61]

Two Levels of Unity

IN ADDITION TO THE ASPECTS of *kavanah* discussed above, that is, *kavanah* directed toward *devekut*, or the aspiration of the worshipper to attach himself to, and merge with, the *En Sof*, there is another, even more sublime aspect of *kavanah*, the purpose of which is to stimulate the "union of the Holy One, blessed be He, with His *Shechinah*." This mystical idea is expressed in a declaration inserted in the Prayer Book,[62] which reads, "For the sake of the union of the Holy One, blessed be He, with His *Shechinah*, in behalf of all Israel."[63]

Now, the whole concept of the *Shechinah* itself, as to what it is, and especially the concept of its union with the "Holy One,

---

60. *Pesachim* 50b; *Nazir* 23b.
61. *Tanya*, chap. 39.
62. Before the so-called *pesukei d'zimra*, in the Morning Liturgy.
63. *Tanya*, chap. 41. This is an abbreviated form of the text that appears in his Siddur.

blessed be He," has often been grossly misunderstood. In the symbolism of the Kabbalah, this "sacred union" is sometimes referred to metaphorically as the union between "King and Queen," or "Bridegroom and Bride," and the like. The uninitiated have often exaggerated this "erotic element" into something akin to the primitive concept of the "sacred marriage." Needless to say, such an idea would be repugnant to our author, as to any true Kabbalist.[64]

It may be debatable whether our author has injected a new meaning into the idea of the *Shechinah*, or whether his interpretation is merely a classical example of ChaBaD dialectic. Be it as it may, his interpretation of the *Shechinah* and its union, not only does away with the "erotic element," but also with much of its underlying mystery.

As usual, the author draws upon the analogy from human experience in order to explain the abstruse ideas connected with his subject. To understand what the *Shechinah* is we must look into ourselves.

The soul, we are told, pervades the entire physical organism from head to foot, yet its principal "habitation" and center of operations is in the brain, whence it extends its influence to all the individual organs of the body. Each organ receives from the soul its own particular vitality which is necessary for the exercise of its sense or function, viz., the eye draws from it its sense of sight, the ear its sense of hearing, the legs the function of walking, and so on. All these senses and functions are also reflected back into the brain through which they operate. Now, the variety of senses and functions that stem from the soul cannot imply an essential multiplicity in the soul itself, which is a simple and indivisible spiritual being, devoid of any physical accidents or properties. It cannot be said, therefore, that the soul, *essentially*, is concentrated more in the brain than in the feet. What can be said, however, is that it *manifests* itself in one organ more than in another, just as the sun can illuminate one room more than another depending upon the amount of light admitted, without any essential variation in the light itself. In this sense it is clear that the soul manifests itself most in the brain, through the fac-

---

64. Cf. *Shomer Emunim* by R. Joseph Ergas (Vilna, 1881), p. 7d.

ulties of *chochmah, binah, da'at* (ChaBaD), the brain sending out, and receiving back, the necessary impulses for each particular organ, including the heart (and for this reason it has been said that the mind has an inherent ascendancy over the heart).[65]

In a somewhat analagous manner the *En Sof* pervades and vitalizes all the supernal and nether worlds, with their infinite number of creatures. Essentially the *En Sof* (as the soul in the illustration) is unknowable and indivisible, and the multiplicity and variety of the worlds and creatures reflect only the degree of *manifestation* of the Infinite Light in them; in other words, the degree of the Divine irradiation that reaches each of them individually. The supernal (spiritual) worlds receive a greater and clearer reflection of the Infinite Light, while the lower worlds receive an inferior quality of Light and Life, which becomes ever more and more obscured and filtered, until it reaches our physical world in such a diminutive state as to be barely perceptible at all behind the dense material screens which conceal the spirit or "soul" of each thing, giving inert objects the appearance of "dead" matter.

To press the analogy further, it has been said that the soul's principal "habitation" is in the brain, through which the soul vivifies each organ of the body. Applying the same principle to the manifestation of the *En Sof*, it, too, expresses itself in terms of the supernal intelligences, namely, the Will, Wisdom, Understanding and Knowledge of the Creator, which are "clothed" in the Torah and its precepts. The manifestation of this general influence is the source of vitality for all things created, each one individually deriving from it its life and existence. This wellspring of Divine Light and Life has been variously called *"alma d'itgalia"* ("Revealed World"), "Matron," "Mother," and *Shechinah*, since it is the origin and source of life for all creatures.[66]

Shechinah is derived from the words *veshachanti betocham*—"I shall dwell among them,"[67] for it is the original radiation of the Divine Light which is revealed in the worlds, and from this source comes the individual degree of

---

65. *Tanya*, chaps. 12, 17, 30, based on *Zohar* III, 224a.
66. *Tanya*, chaps. 35, 41, 51, 52.
67. Exodus 25:8.

light and life to all things (created) in accordance with their due.... The life and light emanating from this source is merely in the form of *radiation*, like the light coming from the sun [which is not the sun itself]; but the *Shechinah* itself—the very origin of the revealed light and its source—which is the source of all existence and life is something that the [finite] worlds are incapable of enduring; for were they to receive the light of the *Shechinah* without its being screened and concealed in a "garment," they would cease to exist, for they would dissolve in their source as the sun's rays at their source are dissolved in the sun itself, since no sunrays can be seen there but the substance of the sun itself. What is this "garment" which can conceal the *Shechinah* and "clothe" it so that the light may be endured without dissolution? It is G-d's Will, Wisdom, etc., which are "clothed" in the Torah and its precepts, revealed to us...and together with [the Torah and precepts] comes the *Shechinah*....[68]

The *Shechinah* is identified with the last sphere of the World of Emanation (*malchut d'Atzilut*), which is the source of the upper spheres of the world next in line, the World of Creation (*Beriah*). By a process of projection from the higher spheres through the lower, and from the higher worlds through the lower, the *Shechinah* "descends" down the line to our own world, in the embodiment of the Torah and its precepts. But in the Torah and its precepts are incorporated the Divine Will and Wisdom, which are infinitely "above" the *Shechinah* (for *chochmah*—wisdom, is the first of the ten *sefirot*, whereas *malchut* is the last). To be sure, the bifurcation of the Infinite Light in the process of creation does not involve a change in the essence of the *En Sof*, as explained.[69] This is affirmed in the daily liturgy, viz., "Thou art He before the world was created, and Thou art He after the world was created." However, in the created world the unity is fractured, resulting in a tremendous gap between the *hidden* and the *revealed*, or, to use the already familiar terms, between *makif* and *memalei*. In the dictionary of Kabbalistic terms and symbols, the

---

68. *Tanya* chap. 52. The passage is quoted here in a somewhat condensed form.
69. In the foregoing chapter.

"Holy One, blessed be He" is the "hidden," and the *Shechinah* is the "revealed," aspect of the *En Sof*, or the "He" (distant) and "Thou" (present), respectively.

This gap, we are told, can be bridged only by the study and practice of the Torah and its precepts which likewise contain both elements, the esoteric and exoteric. Hence the "supernal union" (*yichud elyon*) can be achieved only through the instrumentality of man's Divine service, by means of *kavanah* before and during the performance of the pious acts, whereby man dedicates his acts toward that union. This is the sublimest Divine service, whereby the worshipper not only brings down the *Shechinah* upon himself (i.e., upon his Divine soul and animal soul as well as the physical body, all of which are engaged in the service, mentally, verbally and physically), but he also is instrumental in the diffusion of the Infinite Light in the highest worlds and the realization of the all-embracing union, of the All in All.

It is in this sense that we must understand such "erotic" terms as *yichud* (union) and *zivug* ("coupling") in reference to the spiritual forces. That which is higher acts upon the lower; the first is active, the second is passive; the first "gives," the second "receives." Hence the terms "male" and "female" are used synonymously with efflux and influx. And as in nature, the female stimulates the male, so in Kabbalah it is said that *itaruta d'letata* ("stimulus from below") induces *itaruta d'le'ela* ("stimulus from above") or that the "elevation of feminine waters" brings down the "masculine waters" (water is synonymous with *chesed* grace, influence). All this simply means that by his Divine service man draws upon himself the higher Divine influences, the very *Shechinah* itself.[70]

We have spoken of two forms of "union," the "supernal union" (of the Holy One with His *Shechinah*) and the "lower union" (of man's soul with the *Shechinah*). Hence the two special kinds of *kavanah*. The "lower union," i.e., the union between the human "I" and the Divine "Thou," is easily within reach of the *benoni*, our author tells us, by virtue of the "hidden love" in the soul of every Jew. The more sublime union, however, i.e., the union between the Divine "He" and the Divine "Thou," is more

---

70. *Tanya*, chap. 53.

appropriately within the province of the *tzaddik*, since it is the expression of the highest form of love, which is attained by the *tzaddik* only. Nevertheless, the *benoni*, too, is urged to cultivate the higher *kavanah* as well, even though he lacks that overpowering love of the *tzaddik*, since some element of it is contained in the "hidden love."[71]

---

71. Ibid., chap. 41.

CHAPTER IV

THE FULFILLMENT

Dimensions of Service

In the final analysis *kavanah* is conceived in the *Tanya* in terms of "fear (awe) and love" of G-d which are described in the Zoharitic literature as the "two wings" whereby prayer, the study of the Torah, and all good works "rise" upward to merge with the Unity of G-d. As Rabbi Schneur Zalman explains it, it is the conscious intention to identify one's will with the Will of G-d, and the desire to be absorbed in G-d, that make this "rise" (*aliyah*) and union (*yichud*) possible. Where the religious acts are performed without this intention, but for personal motivations, they cannot rise upward, but remain suspended, as it were, in the world of *kelipot*, until such time as the person repents.

In his familiar way our author amplifies the metaphor of the "wings." The wings are not in themselves vital organs of the bird,[1] yet on them depends the eventual survival of the bird. Similarly, in Divine service, it is the Torah and the commandments which are the essential aspects of the Divine unity, since in them the Supreme Will is revealed; but without the "wings" of fear and love, man's works cannot rise to attain that unity. Moreover, fear and love are also of the 613 commandments, though their essential function is to serve as the ingredients of all the others, or, as the "soul" of all Divine worship.[2]

---

1. *Tanya*, chap. 40. The author cites *Chullin* 56b as his source. This is another instance where the author uses the *halachah* to support his point in the Kabbalah.
2. *Tanya*, chaps. 39, 40.

The fact that fear (awe) of G-d and love of G-d are two commandments indicates that we are dealing with concepts that are
not purely emotional, for how can one be *commanded* to love or
to fear? The commandments merely impose the duty to cultivate
these feelings by means of meditation on the might and majesty
of the *En Sof*. The quality of fear and love experienced by the
individual will thus depend on his mental accomplishment, or on
his *chochmah*, *binah* and *da'at* (ChaBaD).

There is, first of all, the basic fear of G-d which is an essential
attribute to the Divine soul, and is an integral component of the
innate natural love of G-d. This fear is the dread of incurring
G-d's displeasure. To become effective, however, it must be
brought forth from the hidden recesses of the heart by a conscious
effort of contemplation. One must take time, the author tells us, to
reflect upon the omnipotence of the Supreme King, the Creator,
and to cultivate an awareness of being in His presence always, a
special effort being required when directly approaching Him in
service. This is the basic prerequisite of all Divine worship. To start
from love would not be enough, for basically *avodah* ("service")
implies complete subservience, i.e., absolute submission to Divine
authority. This is what is called "accepting the yoke of the
Heavenly Kingdom," as it is interpreted in the *Zohar*[3]. Taking an
analogy from the yoke used for harnessing an animal, the *Zohar*
observes that the function of the yoke is not to afflict the animal,
but rather to steer it in the right direction, and to make it useful
and productive by compliance to its master's will. Analogously, the
"yoke" of the Heavenly Kingdom is not to afflict, but rather to
guide the human being in the right path. Properly cultivated, this
feeling of voluntary submission to the Divine Law transcends any
apprehension of punishment, or any sense of oppression; it rather
gives way to an overwhelming *desire* to do G-d's will, without any
thought of the self. Such "fear" is really a sense of holy awe and
reverence for G-d. Without it, Divine service would be devoid of
holiness. Nevertheless, our author assures us, even if this feeling is
not fully developed, the service is acceptable so long as one is
intent upon serving the Creator with self-surrender.[4]

---

3. *Zohar* III, p. 108a.
4. *Tanya*, chap. 41.

The quality of Divine service motivated by the awe of G-d is spoken of in terms of a servant-master relationship. Its virtue lies in the complete submission and self-surrender of the servant, which is so essential to the mystic union with G-d. But awe is only *one* of the "wings," and essential as it is, it is not enough. There must also be the second "wing," namely, the quality of love, which is characterized by the son-father relationship. Here the feeling of kinship may detract somewhat from the feeling of absolute submission on the part of the son, but this flaw in submission is compensated for by his enthusiasm and eagerness to go beyond the call of duty.

The ideal service is that of the "servant-son," i.e., of the son serving with the quality of a servant. But in order to achieve such perfect service, the basic fear of G-d, which is called *yirah tata'ah* ("lower fear"), will not suffice; it is necessary to cultivate the superior form of fear (*yirah ila'ah*), which goes deeper than the former. For the former is derived from meditation upon the external manifestation of the Divine Majesty in Nature, that is, on the immanence of the Creator (termed *memalei* earlier); hence the awe is also of a more superficial quality. But the more perceptive intellect delves into the subtler aspects of the transcending quality of the Creator (*sovev*), the true Reality, where the resulting affection is that of an overpowering desire for dissolution, in both body and soul, within the All.

Corresponding to the two qualities of fear, or awe, (*yirah tata'ah* and *yirah ila'ah*), there are two qualities of love, *ahavat olam* and *ahava rabbah*.

Ahavat olam is usually translated by "eternal love," but our author, taking the word *olam* in its meaning of "world," translates it by "worldly love." It is the love of G-d derived from contemplation of Nature and the Divine benevolence in it. This love begins with reflection on the world and ends with reflection on G-d in the world, resulting in the realization that all the beauty and wonder of Nature is nothing but the manifestation of the creative power of G-d. Such meditation fosters a sublime and an intense love of G-d, in comparison with which any mundane pleasure, physical or spiritual, pales into insignificance. To quote our author:

By this meditation [on G-d in Nature], the faculty of
love that is in the soul divests itself of its garments, i.e., of
desiring any kind of physical or spiritual enjoyment and
pleasure, or the slightest craving for any mundane thing,
but only for G-d Himself, the source of vitality of all the
pleasures, the source in which they all dissolve into noth-
ingness...as it is written, "Whom have I in heaven but
Thee, and there is none upon earth that I desire with
Thee; my flesh and my heart long for Thee, O G-d, the
strength of my heart, and my portion forever."[5]...He, whose
soul's faculty of love is not clothed at all in any physical or
spiritual enjoyment, is able to inflame his soul as burning
coals, with an intense fire and a flame soaring heavenward....[6]

One way of cultivating love for G-d, "which is suitable for all,"
i.e., within reach of every Jew, Rabbi Schneur Zalman suggests, is
a form of "reciprocal" love, fostered by contemplation of G-d's
love for *this world* and for man in preference to the higher spiritual worlds and the angels. For it is in *this* world, our author
emphasizes, that G-d chose to reveal His will and wisdom by
means of the Torah and the commandments, and it is in *this*
world that He causes His *Shechinah* (Divine Presence) to abide in
a greater measure. Even the angels admit this, the author says,
citing the famous verse, "Holy, holy, holy is the Lord of Hosts, all
the earth is full of His Glory,"[7]—one of the highlights of the daily
liturgy. Thus, reflection on G-d's *ahavat olam* for man's sake must
call forth man's *ahavat olam* for G-d's sake; "as water reflects the
face, so does one heart respond to another."[8]

---

5. Psalms 73:25, 26.
6. *Tanya*, chap. 43. R. Eleazar of Worms wrote in similar terms. The similarity
of language is sometimes striking.
7. Isaiah 6:3.
8. Proverbs 27:19. It is interesting to note how Rabbi Schneur Zalman relates
his thoughts to the liturgy, thereby providing a penetrating commentary on it.
Chapter 49 of the *Tanya*, to which the above paragraph refers, offers a good
example of this method. Incidentally, the discussion provides the explanation
for the change in the text of the prayer beginning with *ahavat olam*, which
Rabbi Schneur Zalman adopted in his Siddur from the Lurianic rite, in contrast
to the Ashkenazic version, *ahavah rabbah*.

There is, however, a more sublime love, called *ahava rabbah* ("abundant love"), or *ahava b'taanugim* (a "love of delights"). It is the purest love which is not attained by meditation, but is bestowed upon the perfect by Divine grace.[9] Because it is an experience of the few, and comes to the *benoni* only in rare moments of sublime communion with G-d, our author does not dwell much on it in the *Tanya*.

We are told, nevertheless, that elements of both qualities of love are to be found, innately and equally, in all Jewish souls, as a heritage from the Patriarchs. We had occasion to meet this concept in earlier chapters of the *Tanya* under the term *ahava mesuteret* ("hidden love"),[10] which is connected with the very essence of the Divine soul. The concept is now amplified to include elements of both *ahava rabbah* and *ahavat olam*.

There is the soul's natural desire for G-d as the source of life. In this sense the *Zohar* interprets the scriptural text, "[Thou art] my soul; I desire Thee in the night";[11] this is the desire for G-d as one desires life itself, for G-d is life. Our author plays on the word "night," speaking of this longing for G-d as the languishing experienced by the weak or tortured person desiring recuperation, or the weary person desiring sleep, in order to wake up refreshed and invigorated.[12] This, however, is a subjective love, a love that desires to be gratified. More sublime by far is the element of innate love in the soul which the *Zohar* describes in terms of selfless filial love, that of the loving son desiring to please his father and mother without any thought of self-gratification, or reward, but out of pure affection, because he loves them more than anything in the world, including his own life. "For He is indeed our true Father."[13]

If, then, the elements of love and fear of G-d are already innately present in the soul of every Jew, the commandments to fear and love G-d, oft repeated in the Torah, make sense. For one

9. *Tanya*, chap. 43; *Iggeret Hakodesh*, chap. 18. Cf. *Zohar* I, 11b.

10. *Tanya*, chaps. 15, 16, 18, 19.

11. Isaiah 26:9. This verse is usually translated "With my soul have I desired Thee," etc. Adopting the Zoharitic interpretation, however, Rabbi Schneur Zalman gives it further depth.

12. *Tanya*, chap. 44.

13. Ibid. Cf. also beg. chap. 2.

is not commanded to excite emotions that are not there, but to awaken and cultivate a natural and deeply rooted attachment. This is the area in which the *Tanya* so insistently emphasizes the importance of meditation and contemplation, as a conscious effort to transform the potential qualities into active and dynamic forces, translated into thought, speech and action of everyday life.

Compassion

THE TWO MAIN DIMENSIONS of Divine service reviewed above, namely, love and awe, on all their levels, are within reach of every Jew, Rabbi Schneur Zalman explains, not only because these attributes are essentially inherent in the Jewish soul, but also because of their hereditary aspect, going back to our Patriarchs.[14] Abraham was the embodiment of the attribute of *chesed* (corresponding to love), and Isaac was the embodiment of *gevurah* (corresponding to awe).[15] The third Patriarch, Jacob, was the embodiment of the attribute of *tiferet* (corresponding to *rachamim*, mercy),[16] introducing the third element of Divine service. How, then, is the attribute of compassion to be evoked and used as a source of inspiration towards a more intensified mode of serving G-d? In other words, how does one serve G-d with compassion?

Let the author speak for himself:[17]

There is yet another direct road open to man, namely, to occupy himself with the Torah and *mitzvot* for their own sake through the attribute of our Patriarch Jacob, peace unto him, this being the attribute of mercy. It is, first, to arouse in his mind great compassion before G-d for the Divine spark which animates his soul that has descended from its Source, the Life of Life, the blessed *En Sof*, Who pervades all worlds and transcends all worlds, and in com-

14. *Tanya*, chaps. 18, 44, etc.
15. *Iggeret Hakodesh*, chaps. 2, 6, 13. Cf. also *Sefer Habahir* 48; *Zohar* I, 41a; II, 51b; III, 131b, etc.
16. *Iggert Hakodesh*, ibid.
17. *Tanya*, chap. 45.

parison with Whom everything is accounted as nothing. Yet this spark has been clothed in a "serpent's skin"[18] which is far removed from the light of the King's countenance, at the greatest possible distance, since this world is the nadir of the coarse *kelipot*, etc.

And especially when he will recall all his actions and utterances and thoughts since the day he came into being, unworthy as they were, causing the King to be "fettered by the tresses"[19]—"by the impetuous thoughts of the brain," for "Jacob in the cord of His inheritance,"[20] as in the illustration of one pulling a rope,[21] and so forth. This is the esoteric doctrine of the "exile of the *Shechinah*." Concerning this it is written, "And let him return unto the Lord, and have mercy upon Him,"[22] arousing great compassion towards G-d Who dwells among us, as it is written, "Who dwelleth among them in the midst of their uncleannesses."[23]....

In this way, a person is able to attain the distinction of *ahava rabbah* ("great love") in the consciousness of his heart, as it is written, "Of Jacob, who redeemed Abraham,"[24] as has been explained elsewhere.[25]

---

18. Cf. *Tikkunei Zohar*, Introduction, 10b; *Etz Chaim*, 49:4; *Pirkei d'R. Eliezer*, chap. 20.

19. Songs 7:6. Another meaning of רהטים is "gutters" (Genesis 30:38). Thus מלך אסור ברהטים could be rendered "A King bound in the gutters." Cf. *Vayikra Rabbah* 31.

20. Deuteronomy 32:9. Note the interpretation of the word חבל, which is usually rendered in this verse and similar contexts as a tract or portion of land (which used to be measured by a rope or cord). The author emphasizes it here in its original meaning, as a metaphor. See following note.

21. Tugging at one end of a rope, vibrates the other end, while pulling the lower end down, brings down also the upper end. The metaphor vividly illustrates the idea that every human act below causes a corresponding reaction On High, as it is often referred to in the phrase *itaruta d'letata* and *itaruta d'le'ela* ("impulse below causes impulse Above"). See also *Iggeret Hateshuvah*, ch. 5.

22. Isaiah 55:7. Note the deviation from the standard translation, "that He (G-d) have mercy upon him (the repenter)." The word וירחמהו permits both renditions.

23. Leviticus 16:16.

24. Isaiah 29:22.

25. *Tanya*, end of chap. 32. *Torah Or*, 51a.

Here we have, in brief, the formulation of the concept of compassion in man's relation to G-d; compassion for the Divine spark and for the *Shechinah* in exile, which can be redeemed and released only through man's service to G-d in the fulfillment of the Torah and *mitzvot*. Moreover, invoking the attribute of compassion serves also as a means of intensifying the quality of love for G-d.

Elsewhere the author considers this attribute as an important first step towards *teshuvah* (repentance). Thus he declares,

> The true and direct path to lower *teshuvah*...is to invoke supreme compassion from the Source of Mercy for his Divine soul, which has fallen from the lofty peak of its Source in the Giver of Life into the deep pit of defilement and *sitra achra*.[26]...

He goes on to explain that through the commission of sin man not only denies himself, but drags into defilement also the Name of G-d, the Divine spark that animates the sinner even during his sinful act. "Therefore the Holy One is called the 'Humiliated King'...for there is no humiliation deeper than this."[27]

The attribute of compassion, like awe and love, is innate in the soul. But, as in the case of the latter, it is necessary to arouse it and bring it down from potentiality to actuality, which calls for contemplation. One must reflect deeply upon the majesty of the Creator and creation so as to become consciously aware of the fact that G-d actually fills heaven and earth down to the lowest detail, in a way that makes it possible for the Divine spark to dwell even in the "dark and gloomy body" which is vulnerable to contamination. But there is the redeeming factor that G-d, in His infinite mercy, gives one the strength to overcome temptation and, in the last resort, the ability to do *teshuvah* and make amends.[28]

Joy

WE HAVE ALREADY NOTED THAT Rabbi Schneur Zalman's main

---

26. *Iggeret Hateshuvah*, chap. 7.
27. Ibid., from *Pirkei Hechalot* and R. Moshe Cordovero.
28. *Iggeret Hakodesh*, chap. 6.

objective in the *Tanya* was to set it up as a "Guide for the Perplexed," which was to serve not so much the sophisticated, as the "average" man. Therefore, he is not content with a theoretical analysis and evaluation of the psychic forces in man. It is not enough, he feels, to tell people that they are intrinsically good, that the forces of light have an inherent advantage over the forces of darkness. He is acutely aware of the tremendous conflicts raging in the average man, not from his personal experience so much, as from the thousands of men who flocked to him for spiritual guidance. So he assumes the role of counsellor, setting forth a detailed plan to help the average man emerge victorious in this great battle between the inner forces of good and evil.

In human combat, the author tells us, sheer physical strength alone is not necessarily the determining factor. The slothful combatant may easily be defeated despite his superior strength. Applying the same principle to the inner conflict between man's two natures, he emphasizes the vital role which is played by the state of mind. Alertness and alacrity are derived from *simchah* (cheerfulness, joy), which requires that the heart be free from oppressive cares and sadness. *Atzvut* (dejection, sadness) dulls the heart and mind and breaks down resistance to temptation. True Divine service can be attained only through *simchah*.[29]

But life is full of cares, worries, and sorrows. How is one to maintain a state of cheerfulness notwithstanding?

Here again the author draws upon the Halachah which he illuminates with the light of the Kabbalah. He quotes the Mishnaic law[30] that it is incumbent on a person to bless G-d for misfortune as well as for good fortune. To him this means more than an exhortation to accept misfortune with resignation. It means that one should actually accept misfortune with joy, as one would welcome a visible and obvious benefit. It is, in fact, a benefit of a *higher* order, higher because it has its origin in the "hidden" worlds which are "above" the revealed order; hence it comes down "in disguise." Thus, the author's subtle conception of "a

---

29. To serve G-d with joy is a Biblical injunction (Deuteronomy 28:47; Psalms 100:2), upon which the Baal Shem Tov had put much emphasis. It is also greatly stressed in the *Zohar* (e.g., II, 165a).
30. *Brachot* 9:5.

blessing in disguise" goes beyond the conventional sense of the phrase, which is the belief that out of the misfortune will eventually come forth some physical good which will more than offset the physical ill; this is something which every faithful person who believes in the essential goodness of the "good Lord" will take for granted. In our author's conception, a "blessing in disguise" is more than that. Misfortune is not merely a means to good fortune in the end; it is already good in itself, for, it is the *spiritual* benefit which he has in mind. This requires explanation. Indeed, Rabbi Schneur Zalman deals with the subject of human affliction at length in his various works. We can only briefly digress here to mention but two: one that touches upon the realm of the esoteric, and one that is more down to earth.

As for the former, the author refers to the Talmudic statement,[31] enumerating several qualities of human response to suffering, one higher than the other: "Those who are humiliated, but do not return the insult" (though they protest!); then there are "those who hear their insult, but do not (even) retort" (i.e., bear it in silence); finally there are "those who perform out of love and are happy with affliction." The Talmud goes on to say, "Concerning them, it is written, 'And they who love Him are like the sun rising in its full strength.'"[32] The metaphor alludes to the gradual rising strength of the sun from sunrise to high noon.

The author follows up the above with the following explanation:

> The reason for rejoicing in physical afflictions is that they are a great and potent favor for the sinning soul, to cleanse it in this world and to redeem it from purification in the next....
>
> Nachmanides, in his Introduction to his Commentary on Job, writes that even the sufferings of Job for seventy years are absolutely of no account in comparison to the soul's suffering even briefly in *Gehinom* (Purgatory).... It is only that this world is built on kindness,[33] and through (comparatively) mild suffering in this world one is saved

---

31. Shab. 88b.
32. Judges 5:31.
33. Psalms 89:3.

from severe judgments in Afterlife. (By way of illustration) the movement of a shadow on earth of a few inches equals the sun's movement in the sky over thousands of miles....[34]

Thus, the truly faithful will not consider personal affliction as "bad"; on the contrary, he considers it in the nature of Divine grace, or, at worst, a "bitter" but life-saving medicine.

On another, "down to earth" level, suffering simply brings one closer to G-d; and proximity to G-d and unity with Him by far outweigh any mundane benefits or blessings that life can hold out for mortal man. Therefore the truly faithful person can be cheerful also in the midst of misfortune or pain.

If, however, sadness connected with mundane affairs should have no place in the life of the *benoni*, what about the sadness that comes with repentance and remorse? Some moralists encourage whatever will intensify an enduring feeling of remorse and repentance. Not so our author. He counsels that such feelings should be reserved for certain propitious moments. They should not be allowed to dominate one's mind constantly, and least of all during prayer, for how could a person then "serve G-d with joy?" And even during those "propitious" moments it should be a case of *merirut* (lit. "bitterness") rather than *atzvut* (dejection) and should soon be replaced by a feeling of relief and joy in the conviction that G-d accepted the sincere repentance of the sinner and has forgiven him. This, in fact, is the truest and fullest kind of joy, the joy of again being near to G-d after having been separated from Him.[35]

There is yet another kind of sadness and melancholy, beside that caused by physical ills and repentance. There is the sadness that comes in the wake of sinful thoughts and temptations, from which none but the *tzaddik* is free. In spite of his best effort to attain purity of mind and thought, the *benoni* cannot preclude a sinful thought from entering his mind. While he is able to dismiss it as soon as it appears, the very fact that he had experienced a temptation, even for a fleeting moment, is likely to arouse a sad feeling in him at the weakness of his flesh. Yet, far from succumbing to any such sadness, even this circumstance, the author

---

34. *Iggeret Hateshuvah*, end of chap. 11 and chap. 12.
35. *Tanya*, chap. 26.

states, can be turned to advantage, if the sinful thought or temptation is considered as a challenge which can effectively be met. Each temptation that is repressed, or sinful thought that is dismissed, serves as a stimulus to greater joy and jubilation in the gratifying feeling of having fulfilled the Divine will and the purpose of Creation. This religious experience is given only to the struggling *benoni*. There is more than the unique religious experience to compensate for the struggle. For the *suppression* of evil and the *conversion* of evil to good are two distinct services and functions. The former can be fulfilled only by the *benoni*, inasmuch as the *rasha*—so long as he remains in that state—has already lost the battle, while the *tzaddik* has already won it and is engaged in a higher form of Divine service, namely, the *conversion* of cosmic evil into good. Thus, even the fact that the *benoni* is destined to experience an inner conflict all his life is no cause for despondency, since this is his Divinely allotted portion.[36]

It is, the author realizes, most exasperating to the sincere worshipper to discover that precisely during prayer he is often confronted by distracting, even sinful, thoughts. Here, too, we find the author has an encouraging word to say. Such an experience is not surprising, he points out, for, as in a combat, it is to be expected that when one side makes a determined effort to gain supremacy, the other side will attempt to match forces. To become upset and frustrated on such an occasion would only play into the hands of the adversary. If all one's efforts to get rid of the distracting thoughts fail, however, there is only one thing left to do: to pray humbly that G-d come to the aid of the embattled Divine soul. This is a prayer that will not be left unanswered, since the Divine soul is a "part" of G-d.[37]

In more extreme cases, however, the author of the *Tanya* makes certain concessions to the moralists who dwell so much on the evil aspects of the animal soul rather than on the sublime qualities of the Divine soul. Where a person finds himself unequal to the battle with his nature, and even during prayer he is unable to "open his heart" which has become as "dull as a stone," he must undertake more stringent measures. The author

36. Ibid., chap. 27.
37. Ibid., chap. 28.

quotes the *Zohar*: "A log that does not catch fire should be splintered; a body into which the light of the soul cannot penetrate must undergo a crushing." This "crushing" means, to the author, a conscious and determined effort to break down one's stony heart by regular periods of introspection, self-reproach, the study of literature conducive to repentance and contrition, making relentless efforts to do more than the minimum, or than that suggested by his natural inclination, in all matters pertaining to his religious activities.[38]

Conspicuously absent from this self-imposed discipline is anything in the way of physical self-castigation, such as fasting or radical austerity. In this respect there is a complete break between the *Tanya* and the older Kabbalah. With Luria[39] the author of the *Tanya* would like to see all forms of *atzvut* banished, even the "worry about sins," except when reciting the daily confession; otherwise, prayer and the study of the Torah should be free from any uneasiness of mind, for "the *Shechinah* only dwells in the midst of joy."[40] Should this recommended discipline lead to a form of *atzvut*, it is nothing alarming, for it is a higher quality of *atzvut* which belongs to the good aspect of *kelipat nogah*, and sometimes it is necessary to use the *kelipah*'s own weapon in order to defeat it.[41] Yet, we are assured that this kind of higher *atzvut* is not the state of dejection so sharply condemned earlier. It is not *atzvut* but *merirut*. The former is identified with a state of inertia, apathy, a dullness and deadness of heart and mind, which are fatal in the inner battle. *Merirut*, on the other hand, is a vital and dynamic force, an essential ingredient of repentance, that leads to *simchah*, as already mentioned. Thus, both *merirut* and *simchah* lie within the realm of holiness, but there is this difference between them: *simchah* is derived from the expansive aspect of *chesed*, hence its

---

38. Ibid., chaps. 29, 30.
39. Emphasis on "Serve G-d with joy" became pronounced in Luria's teachings, in a departure from the tendency of the earlier Kabbalists to accentuate the penitential and sombre mood in Divine service. In one reference to this subject Rabbi Schneur Zalman declares that the Arizal (Rabbi Isaac Luria) attained *ruach hakodesh* (Divine inspiration) by reason of his extraordinary joy in the performance of the *mitzvot*. (*Torah Or*, 22b).
40. *Tanya*, chap. 31.
41. Ibid.

exuberant and extrinsic quality; *merirut* is derived from the stern aspect of *gevurah*, hence its intrinsic severe quality. Both are positive states, and it is sometimes necessary to bring them both into play. But inasmuch as the line of demarcation between *merirut* and *atzvut* is thin, there is the danger of sliding from the first into the second. The author, therefore, cautions to use *merirut* sparingly and reserve it for special occasions, and even then only as a means of quick transition to *simchah*.[42]

Here we are treated, parenthetically, to one of the authors penetrating interpretations of the precepts, in this case the commandment of "Love thy fellow man as thyself."[43] Says he: Where the physical body with its selfish interests is the prime mover in one's life, the individual is separated from G-d as well as from fellow-man; every body is a separate entity and ego. However, where the individual succeeds in transcending his physical boundaries, and the Divine soul becomes his real self, all selfish interests are banished and a sense of true brotherhood unites him with his fellow-man. For all Divine souls are united and absorbed in the G-dhead, and it is only through this common bond that a person experiences true kinship with his fellowman, and the real feeling that there is but one Father to all. Even where the other is sinful, it is still possible to love him by virtue of the good that is within him, i.e., the Divine soul that is temporarily held captive, as it were, by the forces of evil. At any rate, a feeling of compassion for the captive Divine soul should replace any feeling of hatred, for where there is compassion, there can be no hatred.[44]

The author winds up his discussion of the positive psychological factors, which are the defenses of the *benoni* in his inner battle, on a note of *simchah*. He considers it the panacea for a harmonious existence. *Simchah* has to be cultivated by means of periodic contemplation on the unity of G-d. A true conception of this unity illumines and purifies the soul, fortifies it against all temptations and stimulates it to positive action. Moreover, it makes man an integral part of this all-embracing unity. It takes him out of his insignificant existence by providing him with the

---

42. Ibid. Cf. *Iggeret Hakodesh*, chap. 11.
43. Leviticus 19:18.
44. *Tanya*, chap. 32.

key to unlock the mystery of the cosmic order. Thus, man's conduct is no longer a matter of his private concern, or the concern of society; man, alone of all creatures, can justify Creation by making this physical world a fitting "abode" for the Divine *Shechinah*, preparing the ground for the ultimate manifestation of the Divine glory on earth at "the end of days."[45]

The Eschatological Aspect

THE SUBJECT OF ESCHATOLOGY IS ONE of the most obscure in Rabbinic literature. Many and various are the opinions and beliefs expressed by the Rabbis of the Talmud on the subject of life beyond the grave, and they are scattered in various parts of the Talmudic and Midrashic literature. Some of them are doctrinal in nature; others are more in the nature of homilies in which the Rabbis frequently indulged for their psychological effect to encourage virtue and discourage sin. However, out of these various pronouncements certain definite doctrines emerged which commanded general acceptance and became basic tenets of the Jewish faith. These include the survival of the soul, reward and punishment in after-life, the existence of Paradise (*Gan Eden*) and Purgatory (*Gehinom*), the resurrection of the dead, and the "World to Come" (*Olam Haba*).[46] To these must be added the belief in the future Messiah and the Messianic Era, which Maimonides included in his thirteen principles of faith, though strictly speaking the Messianic Era is only a prelude to the "World to Come," not an actual part of it.

Among the reasons which prompted the Rabbis to reveal some knowledge about the Messianic Era or the Hereafter, perhaps the most important one was the fact that it offered a solution to the problem of theodicy. Seeing that in human experience there seems to be no correspondence between virtue and compensation in this life, they concluded that "there is no reward

---

45. Ibid., chaps. 36, 37.
46. The term *Olam Haba*, "World To Come," is sometimes used in reference to *Gan Eden* (Paradise), the abode of pure souls after life on this earth, or in reference to the future world after the Resurrection of the Dead. In Chabad, the term is used in reference to the latter, as will be developed in the course of the discussion.

for the performance of a mitzvah in this world,"[47] and that the real reward and punishment must necessarily come in after-life. This conclusion was reinforced also by the logical necessity of maintaining human freedom. For, obviously, if reward and punishment followed swiftly on the heels of virtue and vice, or even if it were sure to come in a man's lifetime, we would be severely hampered in our freedom and independence of action for we would be acting out of fear or temptation.

It should be noted, finally, that the Rabbis were generally mindful of maintaining a balance between life and after-life. This view is best exemplified in the somewhat enigmatic statement, "Better is one hour of repentance and good works in this world than the whole life of the world to come; and better is one hour of bliss in the world to come than the whole life of this world."[48] This world and the world to come, each possesses a quality not possessed by the other; the two worlds complement each other. But in the final analysis of the Rabbinic view, the goal is the world to come, or, as the author of the above quotation sums it up, "This world is like a vestibule before the world to come: prepare thyself in the vestibule that thou mayest enter into the banqueting hall."[49]

Turning now to Rabbi Schneur Zalman, we may note, first of all, that in his discussions of the Hereafter he is not concerned with the philosophical problems of theodicy and freedom. As a matter of fact, the problem of theodicy does not concern him altogether. The criteria of measuring human happiness which gave rise to the problem are, to his way of thinking, invalid. To him the greatest human pleasure is *devekut*, in the sense of absorption and unity with G-d. Thus virtue and sin already contain within themselves the seeds of reward and punishment in terms of attachment and detachment in relation to G-d, which no earthly pleasure or pain can equal.

Rabbi Schneur Zalman approaches the subject of the Hereafter from an entirely different viewpoint, namely, from his general conception of Creation and human destiny. His view on

---

47. *Kiddushin* 39b. *Chullin* 142a
48. *Avot* 4:17.
49. Ibid., *Mishnah* 16.

the Hereafter is orientated towards *this* world, since, as we have seen, the end of Creation is this physical world, and man's ultimate destiny is linked with it. The Hereafter, too, must in some way be directly linked to this world, and this is precisely what he attempts to do.

If, as we have noted, *devekut*, the feeling of union with G-d, is incomparably greater a pleasure than any worldly good, *hasagah*, the apprehension of the essence of the G-dhead, is indeed the highest reward and pleasure. As our author puts it, "the created intellect can have no enjoyment or pleasure except in what it conceives, understands, knows, and apprehends of the light of the blessed *En Sof*, to the fullest capacity of its understanding and apprehension."[50] In terms of our apprehension, our author points out,[51] the highest reward will come in the time following the Resurrection of the Dead, when the world will have attained its fullest perfection and will shed all its present limitations. Body and soul, too, will have been so purified as to be able to apprehend the essence of the *En Sof*, to a degree infinitely surpassing anything that even pure souls in Paradise are able to comprehend of G-dliness. The process of purification of body and soul, however, must take place here and now, through the performance of the Divine precepts, since it is by means of such actual performance that unity with G-d is attained. At the same time, the performance of the *mitzvot* provides its own reward in this world, too. This is the meaning of the Mishnaic dictum, "the reward of a mitzvah is the mitzvah itself,"[52] that is to say, the experience of proximity and oneness to the *En Sof*.[53] To Rabbi Schneur Zalman, the Rabbinic statement, "there is no reward for a mitzvah in this world," could only mean that there is no reward possible in this physical and limited world for a mitzvah, whose reward is essentially "out of this world."[54]

If we may use a simple analogy by way of illustration, it would be comparable to bestowing a high academic degree, such as

---

50. *Tanya*, chap. 39.
51. Ibid., end chap. 4.
52. *Avot* 4:2.
53. *Tanya*, chaps. 37 and 39.
54. *Iggeret Hakodesh*, chap. 3.

Ph.D., for example, upon a three year old child, whose state of comprehension is limited to a candy or a toy.

Similarly, only infinitely more so, is the difficulty, nay impossibility, of fully comprehending the reward of a Mitzvah in the present world of the senses. For the nature of this reward is the pleasure of *perceiving* the essence of G-d,[55] something we are not able to do with our senses, not only physically but also intellectually; it is simply beyond our imagination. Maimonides expressed it eloquently:

> As the blind man cannot perceive the shade of color, nor the deaf man the strain of sound, so cannot the physical body comprehend the spiritual pleasures (derived in the Hereafter), which are continuous and everlasting and uninterrupted; these pleasures have nothing in common with, nor any relationship whatever to, the pleasure derived from material things. The nature of this pleasure is the conceiving of the essence of the Creator...in the Hereafter, where our souls become wise of the knowledge of the Creator; that pleasure is indivisible, indescribable, and there is nothing that has any semblance to it; it can only be referred to in the words of the prophet when he wished to express his admiration for this eternal joy, "How abundant is Thy goodness!"[56]—this is the eternal good and final purpose (of life on this earth).[57]

We will see later that what Maimonides refers to as *Olam Haba* and final fulfillment is not the same as conceived by Rabbi Schneur Zalman, who follows the tradition of the Kabbalists. However, he would, of course, fully agree with Maimonides on the nature of this reward. Moreover, as a mystic, Rabbi Schneur Zalman allows for a "taste" of *Olam Haba*, or something akin to it, also in the present life.[58] The *tzaddik gamur* experiences it through his ecstatic service; it is the experience of "love with delights";[59]

---

55. Comp. *Kuzari* 1:109, seq.
56. Psalms 31:20.
57. Maimonides, *Commentary on the Mishnah, Sanhedrin*, chap. *Kol Yisrael* (XI). Cf. *Code, Hilchot. Teshuvah* 8:1-3, 6. Albo, *Ikkarim* IV: 31.
58. *Tanya*, chaps. 9, 14.
59. Ibid.; also chaps. 40 and 43. *Iggeret Hakodesh*, chap. 18.

the *benoni*, too, is capable of experiencing it at propitious moments, such as during prayer,[60] or devotional contemplation,[61] or performing a religious duty with the highest degree of *kavanah*. Even the *rasha*, the sinner, can enjoy a taste of this rewarding experience in his own lifetime through the highest form of repentance.[62]

We must now examine Rabbi Schneur Zalman's concept of the Hereafter, the "End of Days," and *Olam Haba*.

In Rabbinic literature "the end of days" mentioned frequently in the Scriptures is conceived in terms of three distinct periods: the Messianic Era, Resurrection, and the World-to-Come.

There is general agreement about the nature of the Messianic Era. This era is formulated clearly by Maimonides in his *Code*.[63] It is described as an era which will see the complete restoration of the Jewish national independence on its own soil, under the reign of a Divinely inspired, but otherwise mortal, King Messiah, a scion of the House of David. Under his reign the Temple (*Bet Hamikdash*) will be rebuilt in Jerusalem, and the Jewish exiles will be gathered in. There will be peace, security and material prosperity, so that everyone will be free to engage in the study of the Torah and the fulfillment of its precepts. According to Maimonides, the prophetic vision "the wolf will dwell with the lamb"[64] is to be understood metaphorically,[65] as an era of universal peace and felicity brought about by the knowledge of G-d, when all the nations of the world "will call upon the name of G-d, to serve Him with one consent."[66] In all other respects the world will continue in its normal natural order (*olam keminhago noheg*).

---

60. *Tanya*, chaps. 12 ff.

61. Ibid., chaps. 14, 16, f.

62. Ibid., chaps. 7, 17, 25.

63. *Hilchot Melachim*, chaps. 11, 12.

64. Isaiah 11:6.

65. On this point, R. Schneur Zalman differs from Maimonides, in that, unlike the latter, he understands the Biblical prophecy in its literal meaning. This is to say, that the nature of the world, including that of the beasts, will be radically changed, so that they will no longer be predators and carnivorous. See R. Menachem Mendel ("Tzemach Tzedek"), *Or Hatorah, Bereishis*, vol. 3, p. 1340. Kehot, 1970, based on a discourse by R. Schneur Zalman, *Et'halech Liozna*, p. 57. (Kehot, 1957).

66. Zephaniah 3:9.

The Messianic Era should not be confused with the *Olam Haba* (the World-to-Come) which, according to Maimonides,[67] is the spiritual world of the souls, to which the purified intellects will return after the Era of the Resurrection. It is a world of unimaginable spiritual bliss, the nature of which is the pure knowledge of G-d, as quoted above. This opinion is consistent with his general view that angels are superior beings to humans,[68] and that the greatest attainment to which humans can aspire is to eventually dwell in a world of pure spirit and intelligence.

Nachmanides,[69] on the other hand, while agreeing that the ultimate reward and pleasure will be of the nature described by his predecessor, maintains that the era of the Resurrection is the final *Olam Haba*, after which there will be no death, and that reward and pleasure will be enjoyed by the soul as it informs the physical body, which, however, will require no physical food or drink, as it will be sustained by the Divine influence, in the way Moses was sustained during his forty days on Mount Sinai.

On this question, our author takes the view of Nachmanides, because it is also the view of the Kabbalah.[70]

Paradise is only a temporary spiritual abode for the soul after its life on earth. The Resurrection is the culmination point of Creation, and it will infinitely surpass in Divine revelation, as well as in the apprehension of the *En Sof*, the utmost degree of such revelation and apprehension which is possible in the supernal worlds of the spirit. We have already seen how our author explains the seeming anomaly that there could be a greater degree of communion with G-d while the soul is clothed in a body than when it is free from it. In the highest worlds also, the Infinite Light is "screened," as otherwise they could not endure it and could not have a separate existence. Besides, a soul is something created, and no created being, even the highest angels, can conceive the essence of the Creator. However, the study of the Torah and the performance of the precepts, while the soul still

---

67. *Code, Hilchot Teshuvah*, chaps. 8, 9.
68. *Guide*, II, 6, 11.
69. *Shaar Hagemul*.
70. *Derech Mitzvotecha*, by Rabbi Menachem Mendel of Lubavitch. (Kehot, 1953), p. 146. Cf. also *Shnei Luchot Habrit*. 12a f.; 22b f; 385a.

informs the body, enable man to attain the greatest Divine influence, wherewith both his body and soul are permeated and "conditioned," as it were, to endure the ultimate in Divine revelation, without any screens whatever. This will be the "world-to-come" that will be ushered in with the Resurrection, when the world will have reached its highest perfection for which it had been created.[71]

The Mystical Aspect

THE TANYA REPRESENTS A NEW APPROACH to the interpretation of Jewish ethics and theology. It marks an attempt to formulate a system which, while retaining all the basic elements of the traditional Jewish concepts, would be rooted in the mystic discipline of the Kabbalah. To put it in another way, Rabbi Schneur Zalman endeavored to integrate some basic doctrines of the Kabbalah (primarily of the Lurianic school) into the Jewish way of life through a process of reinterpretation. This he accomplished by reducing some highly abstruse Kabbalistic ideas to rational categories, making them more comprehensible by the ample use of illustration and analogy from human experience. The resulting system might well be described as an ethics based on "rational mysticism," paradoxical though this term may be.

Rabbi Schneur Zalman, as we have had occasion to note,[72] had experienced mystic communion and ecstasy of a high order. In the *Tanya* we find the familiar language of mysticism, in terms often reaching considerable refinement. Consider, for example, the variety of loves which the author describes: *ahava mesuteret*, *ahavat olam*, *ahava rabbah*, *ahava b'taanugim*, which received some attention in the previous pages. Then there are additional distinctions which the author makes in the emotional quality of these loves: the calm, nostalgic longing, symbolized by "silver,"[73] and the stormy, passionate, and fiery love symbolized by "gold," which generates in the soul a painful "thirst," developing into a

---

71. *Tanya*, chaps. 36, 37. *Iggeret Hakodesh*, chap. 17.
72. Mindel, *Rabbi Schneur Zalman of Liadi* vol. 1, pp. 61-2.
73. The Hebrew word *kesef* means both "silver" and "longing" (as in, e.g., Genesis 31:30).

state of "lovesickness." The pinnacle of ecstasy is reached when the soul seems ready to take flight from the body in its all-consuming longing for the mystic union.[74]

However, the ecstasy described in the *Tanya* does not culminate in a state of nirvana, nor in a state of frustration and despair, the so-called "dark night" of recession, of which Hindu and Christian mystics speak. There is nothing of the one nor of the other in the mysticism of the *Tanya*. Here the "advance and retreat" (*ratzo v'shuv*)[75] of mystic experience is of an entirely different nature from that described as the "flow and ebb," or "impetus and recession" of other mystic disciplines. In the *Tanya* it is conceived as a mutually complementary process between contemplation and action, since contemplation must be consummated in action. Action completes the mystic union. The advance and retreat of the *Tanya* mysticism are not antithetical; on the contrary, they are conceived, metaphorically speaking, as the harmonious "breathing" of the soul, or the rhythmic pulsation of its "heart." Indeed, there can be a quickening of the pace, but the harmony and rhythm are not disturbed thereby, since each deeper inhalation must result in a more sustained exhalation, and vice versa. Here, again, the human being, the *microcosm*, meets the *macrocosm*, for the latter, too, is conceived as a unified organism "breathing" and "pulsating" with a harmonious vitality.

If the *Tanya's* conception of the "advance and retreat" of the *microcosm* comes close to Neoplatonic thought, that "procession and reversion together constitute a single movement, the diastole-systole, which is the life of the universe," it is here also that the *Tanya* radically diverges from it. In Neoplatonism the human soul must forever strive to get away from the evil regions of matter. There is nothing that the spirit can derive from matter. "The inferior cannot act upon the superior." Not so in ChaBaD where matter is primarily viewed as neutral. Man can make matter a powerful instrument of the spirit. Indeed, it is only when he uses matter as a vehicle for the spirit that he can realize his full capacities and fulfill his destiny. Man is, after all, a creature of matter and spirit, and both must play their part in the fulfillment of this

74. *Tanya*, chap. 50.
75. Ibid., chaps. 41, 50.

destiny. It is in this *material* world where the final act of the dramatic mystery of life unfolds itself. To quote the author:

> It is written in *Sefer Yetzirah*, "If thy heart hasteneth, return to the One." The meaning of the phrase "if thy heart hasteneth" is the craving of the soul...when it expands and bursts into a flame, growing so exceedingly passionate that it is on the very verge of expiration, ready to pour itself into the lap of its Father, the blessed Giver of life, and to liberate itself from its confinement in the corporeal and physical body, in order to attach itself to Him, blessed be He. At this moment, one must recall to heart the teaching of the Rabbis, of blessed memory, "Perforce dost thou live"[76] in this body, animating it for the purpose of drawing down below the higher life from the blessed Giver of life, through the Torah of life, so that there may be an abode for His blessed Unity in the lower world in a manifest manner.... And this is the interpretation of the text, "Come my beloved," etc.[77]

The full text of the verse is, "Come, my beloved, let us go forth into the field; let us lodge in the villages."[78] The "field" and the "villages" are allegorically understood as our gross material world, and it is here and now where the union of lover and beloved is to be consummated, and this world is made a fitting "abode" for both man and G-d—through the fulfillment of the Torah and *mitzvot* in the day-to-day life.

It is on this mystical yet very much down-to-earth note that Rabbi Schneur Zalman concludes his ChaBaD system in the *Tanya.*

---

76. *Avot* 4:22.
77. *Tanya*, chap. 50.
78. Song of Songs 7:22.

SUPPLEMENT

SELECTED READINGS FROM LIKKUTEI AMARIM—TANYA
(PART ONE)

Note:

The sources quoted at the end of each passage refers to the pagination in the Bi-Lingual, Hebrew-English edition of *Tanya*, published by Kehot Publication Society. The footnotes, however, have been adjusted to run consecutively for each section, and subtitles have been provided for these readings.

TWO SOULS

The Animal Soul

IN THE LIGHT OF WHAT Rabbi Chaim Vital wrote in *Shaar Hakedushah* (and in *Etz Chaim*, Portal 50, ch. 2) every Jew, whether righteous or wicked, possesses two souls, as it is written, "The *neshamot* (souls) which I have made,"[1] [alluding to] two souls. There is one soul which originates in the *kelipah*[2] and *sitra achra*[3] and which is clothed in the blood of a human being, giving life to the body, as is written, "For the life of the flesh is in the blood."[4] From it stem all the evil characteristics deriving from the four evil elements which are contained in it. These are: anger and pride, which emanate from the element of Fire, the nature of which is to rise upwards; the appetite for pleasures—from the element of Water, for water makes to grow all kinds of enjoyment; frivolity and scoffing, boasting and idle talk—from the element of Air; and sloth and melancholy—from the element of Earth. From this soul stem also the good characteristics which are to be found in the innate nature of all Israel, such as mercy and benevolence. For in the case of Israel, this soul of the *kelipah* is derived

---

1. Isaiah 57:16.
2. *Kelipah*, "bark," or "shell," the symbol frequently used in Kabbalah to denote "evil" and the source of sensual desires in human nature (*Zohar* I, 19b; II, 69b, 198b, 184a; III, 185a, etc.). Often mentioned together with *sitra achra* (v.).
3. *Sitra achra*, "the other side," i.e. not the side of holiness; it is another term for "evil" in that it negates the G-dhead. Anything that tends to separate from G-d belongs in the *sitra achra*, the root of evil.
4. Leviticus 17:11.

from *kelipat nogah*,[5] which also contains good, as it originates in the esoteric "Tree of Knowledge of Good and Evil."[6]

[*Tanya*, ch. 1, pp. 3-5.]

The Divine Soul

THE SECOND SOUL OF A JEW is truly a part of G-d above,[1] as it is written, "and He breathed into his nostrils the breath of life,"[2] and "Thou didst breathe it [the soul] into me."[3] And it is written in the *Zohar*, "He who exhales, exhales from within him," that is to say, from his inwardness and his innermost, for it is something of his internal and innermost vitality that man emits through breathing out with force.

So, allegorically speaking, have the souls of Jews risen in the [Divine] thought,[4] as it is written, "My firstborn son is Israel,"[5] and "Ye are children unto the Lord your G-d."[6] That is to say, just as a child is derived from his father's brain, so—to use an anthropomorphism—the soul of each Israelite is derived from G-d's (blessed be He) thought and wisdom. For He is wise—but not through a knowable wisdom,[7] because He and His wisdom are one; and as Maimonides says that "He is the Knowledge and the Knower, etc., and this is not within the power of any man to comprehend clearly,"[8] etc., as it is written, "Canst thou by searching

---

5. *Kelipat nogah*, "translucent shell," contains some good, as distinguished from the three completely "dark" *kelipot* containing no good at all. The term is based on an interpretation of the "brightness" (*nogah*) in Ezekiel's vision (1:4). The "animal soul" (*nefesh habahamit*) in the Jew is derived from *kelipat nogah*, by contrast to his "divine soul" (*nefesh elokit*) which is "part" of G-dliness. (Chaps. 1, 7, 37, 40).
6. Cf. *Zohar* I, 12b.

1. Job 31:2; cf. also Psalms 16:5, 73:26; Jeremiah 10:16.
2. Genesis 2:7; comp. Nachmanides' Commentary, *ad loc.*
3. Liturgy, Morning Prayer. *Brachot* 60b.
4. Cf. *Bereshit Rabbah* 1:4.
5. Exodus 4:22.
6. Deuteronomy 14:1.
7. Introduction to *Tikkunei Zohar* 17b.
8. Code, *Hilchot Yesodei Hatorah* 2:10.

find G-d?"[9] And it is also written, "For My thoughts are not your thoughts,"[10] etc.

And though there are myriads of different gradations of souls (*neshamot*), rank upon rank, *ad infinitum*, as with the superiority of the souls of the Patriarchs and of Moses our Teacher above the souls of our own generations who live in the period preceding the coming of the Messiah, which are as the very soles[11] of the feet compared with the brain and head, so in every generation there are the leaders of the Jews, whose souls are in the category of "head" and "brain" in comparison with those of the masses and the ignorant. Likewise [are there distinctions between] *nefashot* and *nefashot*, for every soul consists of *nefesh*, *ruach* and *neshamah*.[12] Nevertheless, the root of every *nefesh*, *ruach* and *neshamah*, from the highest of all ranks to the lowest that is embodied within the illiterate and the most worthless, all derive, as it were, from the Supreme Mind which is *Chochmah Ila'ah* (Supernal Wisdom).[13]

[*Tanya*, ch. 2, pp. 5-7.]

THE SOUL'S FACULTIES: CHABAD

NOW, EACH DISTINCTION AND GRADE of the three—*nefesh*, *ruach* and *neshamah*—consists of[1] ten faculties, corresponding to the Supernal ten *sefirot* (Divine manifestations),[2] from which they

---

9. Job 11:7.

10. Isaiah 55:8.

11. A play on the word עקבתא "soles."

12. Cf. *Zohar* I, 206a; II, 141b, etc.; also *Shnei Luchot Habrit* I, 9b. See also p. 31 f. above.

13. *Chochmah Ila'ah*, "Supernal Wisdom," the first of the ten supernal *sefirot*; the attribute of *chochmah* in *Atzilut*.

1. Elsewhere (e.g., *Likkutei Torah*, *Bamidbar* 1a, 51b; *Shir Hashirim* 16d) the author makes it clear that the soul does not "consist" of the ten faculties but rather manifests itself through them, since the soul itself is essentially unknowable.

2. The ten *sefirot* are more fully discussed by the author in the fourth part of the book, *Iggeret Hakodesh*, ch. 15 and elsewhere.

have descended, which are subdivided into two, namely, the three "mothers" and the seven "multiples," to wit: *chochmah* (wisdom), *binah* (understanding), and *da'at* (knowledge); and the "seven days of Creation:" *chesed* (kindness), *gevurah* (power), *tiferet* (beauty), etc.[3]

Similarly is it with the human soul, which is divided in two—*sechel* (intellect) and *middot* (emotional attributes). The intellect includes *chochmah*, *binah* and *da'at* (ChaBaD), whilst the *middot* are love of G-d, dread and awe of Him, glorification of Him, etc. ChaBaD [the intellectual faculties] are called "mothers" and source of the *middot*, for the latter are "offspring" of the former.

The explanation of the matter is as follows:

The intellect of the rational soul, which is the faculty that conceives any thing, is given the appellation of *chochmah*—כ"ח מ"ה—the "potentiality" of "what is."[4] When one brings forth this power from the potential into the actual, that is, when [a person] cogitates with his intellect in order to understand a thing truly and profoundly as it evolves from the concept which he has conceived in his intellect, this is called *binah*. These [*chochmah* and *binah*] are the very "father" and "mother" which give birth to love of G-d, and awe and dread of Him. For when the intellect in the rational soul deeply contemplates and immerses itself exceedingly in the greatness of G-d, how He fills all worlds and encompasses all worlds,[5] and in the presence of Whom everything is considered as nothing[6]—there will be born and aroused in his mind and thought the emotion of awe for the Divine Majesty, to fear and be humble before His blessed greatness, which is without end or limit, and to have the dread of G-d in his heart. Next, his heart will glow with an intense love, like burning coals, with a passion, desire and longing, and a yearning soul, towards the greatness of the blessed *En Sof*. This constitutes the culminating passion of the soul, of which Scripture speaks, as "My soul longeth, yea, even

---

3. Ibid.
4. *Zohar* III, 28a, 34a. A play on the Hebrew word חכמה—כ"ח מ"ה. It is also to be understood as "pure" or "creative" reason *in potentia*.
5. I.e. both immanently and transcendently. *Zohar* III, 225a.
6. *Zohar* I, 11b.

faineth,"[7] etc., and "My soul thirsteth for G-d,"[8] etc., and "My soul thirsteth for Thee,"[9] etc. The rest of the *middot* are all offshoots of fear and love and their derivations, as is explained elsewhere.

Da'at, the etymology of which is to be found in the verse: "And Adam knew (*yada*) Eve,"[10] implies attachment and union. That is, one binds his mind with a very firm and strong bond to, and firmly fixes his thought on, the greatness of the blessed *En Sof*, without diverting his mind [from Him]. For even one who is wise and understanding of the greatness of the blessed *En Sof*, will not—unless he binds his knowledge and fixes his thought with firmness and perseverance—produce in his soul true love and fear, but only vain fancies. Therefore *da'at* is the basis of the *middot* and the source of their vitality; it contains *chesed* and *gevurah*, that is to say, love with its offshoots and fear with its offshoots.[11]

[*Tanya*, ch. 3, pp. 9-11.]

THE SOULS GARMENTS

IN ADDITION,[1] EVERY DIVINE SOUL (*nefesh elokit*) possesses three garments, viz., thought, speech and action, [expressing themselves] in the 613 commandments of the Torah. For, when a person *actively*[2] fulfills all the precepts which require physical action,[3] and with his power of *speech* he occupies himself in expounding all the 613 commandments and their practical appli-

---

7. Psalms 84:3.
8. Ibid. 42:3.
9. Ibid. 63:2.
10. Genesis 4:1.
11. Love and fear (awe) are two basic emotions latent in the soul which are produced by contemplation. The faculty of *da'at* stimulates these higher emotions to seek an outlet through the three "garments" of the soul, discussed in the following chapter.

1. Having outlined in ch. 3 the intrinsic faculties of the soul, the author goes on to explain how they express themselves through the three outer "garments," or instruments.
2. All italics are the translator's.
3. Note that "action" is put first.

cation, and with his power of *thought* he comprehends all that is comprehensible to him in the *Pardes*[4] of the Torah—then the totality of the 613 "organs" of his soul[5] are clothed in the 613 commandments of the Torah.

Specifically: the faculties of ChaBaD in his soul are clothed in the comprehension of the Torah, which he comprehends in *Pardes*, to the extent of his mental capacity and the supernal root of his soul. And the *middot*, namely fear and love, together with their offshoots and ramifications, are clothed in the fulfillment of the commandments in deed and in word, namely, in the study of Torah which is "the equivalent of all the commandments."[6] For love is the root of all the 248 positive commands, all originating in it and having no true foundation without it, inasmuch as he fulfills them in truth who truly loves the name of G-d and desires to cleave to Him in truth; for one cannot truly cleave to Him except through the fulfillment of the 248 commandments which are the 248 "organs of the King,"[7] as it were, as is explained elsewhere;[8] whilst fear is the root of the 365 prohibitive commands, fearing to rebel against the Supreme King of kings, the Holy One, blessed be He; or a still deeper fear than this—when he feels ashamed in the presence of the Divine greatness to rebel against His glory and do what is evil in His eyes, namely, any of the abominable things hated by G-d, which are the *kelipot* and *sitra achra*, which draw their nurture from man below and have their hold in him through the 365 prohibitive commands [that he violates].

[*Tanya*, ch. 4, pp. 13.]

---

4. Literally meaning "orchard," it is taken as an acrostic of the four Hebrew words פשט, רמז, דרוש, סוד, meaning: plain sense, intimation, homiletical exposition and esoteric meaning, respectively, the four levels of Scriptural interpretation.

5. The physical organism of the human body consists of 248 members and 365 blood vessels, corresponding to the 248 positive and 365 prohibitive commands (*Tanchuma Hakadum, Tetzei*; *Makkot* 24a). The soul, contains the spiritual counterparts of these 613 "organs." (See ch. 51, below.)

6. Mishnah, Peah 1:1.

7. *Tikkunei Zohar, Tikkun* 30.

8. Infra, ch. 23.

FOOD AND GARMENTS OF THE SOUL

SINCE, IN THE CASE OF knowledge of the Torah, the Torah is clothed in the soul and intellect of a person, and is absorbed in them, it is called "bread" and "food" of the soul. For just as physical bread nourishes the body as it is absorbed internally, in his very inner self, where it is transformed into blood and flesh of his flesh, whereby he lives and exists—so, too, it is with the knowledge of the Torah and its comprehension by the soul of the person who studies it well, with a concentration of his intellect, until the Torah is absorbed by his intellect and is united with it and they become one. This becomes nourishment for the soul, and its inner life from the Giver of life, the blessed *En Sof*, Who is clothed in His wisdom and in His Torah that are [absorbed] in it [the soul].

[*Tanya*, ch. 5, pp. 19-21.]

"THE ALMIGHTY HAS CREATED ONE THING OPPOSITE THE OTHER."[1] Just as the divine soul consists of ten holy *sefirot* and is clothed in three holy garments,[2] so does the soul which is derived from the *sitra achra* of the *kelipat nogah*, which is clothed in man's blood, consist of ten "crowns of impurity."[3] These are the seven evil *middot* which stem from the four evil elements mentioned above,[4] and the intellect begetting them which is subdivided into three, viz., wisdom, understanding and knowledge, the source of the *middot*.[5] For the *middot* are according to the quality of the intellect. Hence a child desires and loves petty things of inferior worth, for his intellect is too immature and deficient to appreciate things that are much more precious. Likewise is he provoked

---

1. Ecclesiastes 7:14. In general, things in the realm of holiness have their opposite in the realm of the profane, or "the other side" (*sitra achra*). Similarly, everything in the physical world has its spiritual counterpart from which it derives its existence and vitality—a popular concept in Chabad, as in Kabbalah generally. Cf. *Zohar* III, 47b.
2. Thought, speech, and deed.
3. Cf. *Zohar* III, 41a, 70a.
4. End of ch. 1.
5. Here, unlike ch. 3, the *middot* precede *sechel* to indicate the secondary role of the intellect in the animal soul, where passion predominates.

to anger and vexation over trivial things; so, too, with boasting and other *middot.*

Now these ten unclean categories, when a person meditates in them or speaks them, or acts by them, his thought—which is in his brain; and his speech—which is in his mouth; and the power of action—which is in his hands, together with his other limbs—all these are called the "impure garments" of these ten unclean categories wherein the latter are clothed at the time of the action, speech, or thought. It is these that constitute all the deeds that are done under the sun, which are all "vanity and striving after the wind,"[6] as interpreted in the *Zohar, Beshalach,*[7] in the sense of a "ruination of the spirit,"[8] etc.

So, too, are all utterances and thoughts which are not directed towards G-d and His will and service. For this is the meaning of *sitra achra*—"the other side," i.e. not the side of holiness. For the holy side is nothing but the indwelling and extension of the holiness of the Holy One, blessed be He, and He dwells only on such thing that abnegates itself completely to Him, either actually, as in the case of the angels above, or potentially, as in the case of every Jew down below, having the capacity to abnegate himself completely to the Holy One, blessed be He, through martyrdom for the sanctification of G-d.

[*Tanya*, ch. 6, pp. 21-23.]

THE INNER BATTLE

THE ABODE[1] OF THE ANIMAL SOUL (*nefesh habahamit*) derived from the *kelipat nogah* in every Jew, is in the heart, in the left ventricle that is filled with blood. It is written, "For the blood is the *nefesh.*"[2] Hence all lusts and boasting and anger and similar passions are in the heart, and from the heart they spread throughout

---

6. Ecclesiastes 1:14.
7. II, p. 59a.
8. A reinterpretation of רעות רוח.

1. In the sense of its principal area of manifestation.
2. Deuteronomy 12:23. Cf. Supra, end of ch. 1. Nefesh means life, and also "desire" (Genesis 23:8).

the whole body, rising also to the brain in the head, so as to think and meditate about them and become cunning in them,[3] just as the blood has its source in the heart and from the heart it circulates into every limb, rising also to the brain in the head.

But the abode of the divine soul is in the brains[4] that are in the head, and from there it extends to all the limbs; and also in the heart, in the right ventricle wherein there is no blood, as is written, "The heart of the wise man is on his right."[5] It is [the source of] man's fervent love towards G-d which, like flaming coals, flares up in the heart of discerning men who understand and reflect, with the [faculty of] knowledge[6] of their brain, on matters that arouse this love;[7] also [of] the gladness of the heart in the beauty of G-d and the majesty of His glory [which is aroused] when the eyes of the wise man, that are in his head,[8] i.e. in the brain harboring his wisdom and understanding, gaze at the glory of the King and the beauty of His greatness that are unfathomable and without end or limit, as explained elsewhere; as also the other holy affections (*middot*) in the heart originate from ChaBaD [wisdom, understanding, knowledge] in the brains.

It is written, however, "One nation shall prevail over the other nation."[9] The body is called a "small city."[10] Just as two kings wage war over a town, which each wishes to capture and rule, that is to say, to dominate its inhabitants according to his will, so that they obey him in all that he decrees for them, so do the two souls—the divine and the vitalizing animal soul that comes from the *kelipah*—wage war against each other over the body and all its limbs. It is the desire and will of the divine soul that she alone rule over the person and direct him, and that all his limbs should obey her and surrender themselves completely to

3. The animal soul is mainly moved by passion, while the intelligence reacts to it.
4. The divine soul is essentially intellective.
5. Ecclesiastes 10:2.
6. For the term *da'at* ("knowledge"), see end ch. 3, above.
7. In the divine soul the relation between mind and heart is reversed from that of the animal soul. (See n. 3, above.)
8. Comp. Ecclesiastes 2:14.
9. Genesis 25:23.
10. Ecclesiastes 9:14; *Nedarim* 32b.

her and become a vehicle[11] for her, as well as a robe [instrument] for her ten faculties and three garments mentioned above,[12] all of which should pervade the organs of the body, and the entire body should be permeated with them alone, to the exclusion of any alien influence, G-d forbid. That is to say, that the three brains[13] that are in the head shall be permeated with ChaBaD of the divine soul, namely, the wisdom of G-d and the understanding of Him, by pondering on His unfathomable and infinite greatness; and from them shall be born, through the *da'at* (knowledge),[14] awe in his mind and dread of G-d in his heart,[15] as well as love of G-d that shall flare up like a glowing fire in his heart, like flaming coals, so that his soul shall yearn and long, with passion and desire, to cleave to the blessed *En Sof*, with his whole heart, soul and might, from the very depths of the right ventricle of the heart. The latter would be so thoroughly permeated with love to overflowing, as to inundate the left side as well, to the extent of subduing the *sitra achra* with its element of the "evil waters," namely, the lust stemming from *kelipat nogah*, changing it and transforming it from seeking the pleasures of this world to the love of G-d. Thus it is written, " 'With all thine heart'[16]—with both your natures."[17] That is to say, that the person shall steadily rise to attain to the degree of "abundant love," a supreme affection surpassing that of "ardent love" that is comparable to burning coals.[18] This is what is called in Scripture "love of delights,"[19] which is the experience of delight in G-dliness, of the nature of

---

11. An instrument without independent will.

12. Chaps. 3 and 4.

13. The three intellectual faculties *chochmah*, *binah*, and *da'at*— ChaBaD—have their corresponding physical brains.

14. See note 6, above.

15. Awe is regarded as a preliminary to love. There is, however, a higher category of reverence which can be attained only after having attained love.

16. Numbers 6:5.

17. *Brachot* 54a.

18. The author distinguishes various degrees of love: *ahavah azah* ("ardent" love)—a passionate love, and *ahavah rabbah* ("great" love) or *ahavah beta'anugim* ("delightful" love)—a serene love of fulfillment. The first is likened to a burning flame; the second—to calm waters. These and other distinctions of love are later discussed at greater length. Cf. Chaps. 15, 16, 18, 40, 41, 46, 49.

19. Song of Songs 1:1.

the world to come. This delight is in the brain of wisdom, in the intellectual pleasure of comprehending and knowing G-d, to the extent that one's intellect and wisdom can grasp [Him]. This is the element of "water," and "seed," i.e., light that is sown in the holiness of the divine soul that converts to good the element of "water" in the animal soul, from which the lust for mundane pleasures had been previously derived.[20]

Thus it is written in *Etz Chaim*, Portal 50, ch. 3, on the authority of the *Zohar*, that the evil is converted into, and becomes, completely good, like the good nature itself, through the shedding of the soiled garments, the pleasures of this world, in which it had been clothed.

So, too, shall the other *middot* in the heart, the offshoots of awe and love, be dedicated to G-d alone; and the faculty of speech that is in his mouth, and the thought that is in his mind, shall be entirely and solely the instruments of the "garments" of thought and speech of the divine soul alone, namely, meditation on G-d and His Torah, which shall be the theme of his speech throughout the day, his mouth ceaselessly studying [it]; and the faculty of action centered in his hands, as also in the rest of the 248 organs, shall function exclusively in the performance of the commandments, which is the third garment of the divine soul.

However, the desire of the animal soul which is derived from the *kelipah* is the very opposite—and it is for the good of man, that he may prevail over her and vanquish her, as in the parable of the harlot in the holy *Zohar*.[21]

[*Tanya*, ch. 9.]

---

20. Thus the divine soul is conceived as being potentially capable of not only suppressing the evil impulse, but also completely "sublimating" it.

21. See also end of ch. 29. The parable: A king desired to test the moral strength of his only son. He had a most charming and clever woman brought before him. Explaining to her the purpose of the test, he ordered her to try her best to seduce the crownprince. For the test to be valid, the "harlot" had to use all her charms and guile, without betraying her mission in the slightest way. Any imperfection on her part would mean disobedience and failure of her mission. While the "harlot" uses all her seductive powers, she inwardly desires that the crownprince should not succumb to them. Cf. *Zohar* II, p. 163a.

This parable is intended to explain the ultimate function of the animal soul,

THE BENONI

THE "INTERMEDIATE MAN" (*benoni*) is he in whom evil never attains enough power to capture the "small city," so as to clothe itself in the body and make it sin. That is to say, the three "garments" of the animal soul, namely, thought, speech and act, originating in the *kelipah*, do not prevail with him over the divine soul to the extent of clothing themselves in the body—in the brain, in the mouth and in the other 248 parts[1]—thereby causing them to sin and defiling them, G-d forbid.

Only the three garments of the divine soul, they alone, are implemented in the body, being the thought, speech and act engaged in the 613 commandments of the Torah. He has never committed, nor ever will commit, any transgression; neither can the name "wicked" be applied to him even temporarily, or even for a moment, throughout his life.[2]

However, the essence and being of the divine soul, which are its ten faculties,[3] do not constantly hold undisputed sovereignty and sway over the "small city," except at appropriate times, such as during the recital of the *Shema* or the *Amidah*, which is a time when the Supernal Intellect is in a sublime state;[4] and likewise below, this is a propitious time for every man, when he binds his ChaBaD (intellectual faculties) to G-d, to meditate deeply on the greatness of the blessed *En Sof*, and to arouse the burning love

---

with its inherent evil and complete license and independence. Yet although the forces of evil must be real enough for the purpose of which they have been created, their origin and purpose is rooted in good, and they can, in fact, be so converted. Herein lies the underlying principle of the problem of evil.

1. "Brain"—*thought*; "mouth"—*word*; "the other limbs"—*act*.
2. Though the *benoni* has never committed a sin in his life, he is still not deemed a *tzaddik*, as long as his natural impulses have not been completely sublimated, as explained further in this chapter. On the other hand, past offences need not preclude one from attaining the rank of *benoni*, if there was proper repentance. At any rate, the rank of *benoni*, as defined in the *Tanya*, is far superior to the rank of *tzaddik* as defined generally when it is applied to one whose good deeds exceed the bad.
3. Supra, ch. 3.
4. מוחין דגדלות i.e. the Supernal *Sefirot* of chochmah, binah, da'at (ChaBaD), are in a state of expansion.

in the right part of his heart, to cleave to Him by virtue of the fulfillment of the Torah and its commandments out of love.... At such time the evil that is in the left part is subjected to, and nullified in, the goodness that is diffused in the right part, from the wisdom, understanding and knowledge (ChaBaD) in the brain, which are bound to the greatness of the blessed En Sof.[5]

However, after prayer, when the state of sublimity of the Intellect of the blessed En Sof departs, the evil in the left part reawakens, and he begins to feel a desire for the lusts of the world and its delights. Yet, because the evil has not the sole authority and dominion over the "city," it is unable to carry out this desire from the potential into the actual by clothing itself in the bodily limbs, in actual deed, speech and thought; not to concentrate attention on the enjoyment of the mundane pleasures, as to how to satisfy the lust of his heart, because the brain rules over the heart (as explained in Ra'aya Mehemna, Parshat Pinchas)[6] by virtue of its innately created nature. For this is how man is created from birth, that each person may, with the will-power in his brain, restrain himself and control the drive of lust that is in his heart, preventing his heart's desires from expressing themselves in action, word or thought, and divert his attention altogether from the craving of his heart toward the completely opposite direction, particularly in the direction of holiness.[7]

Thus it is written: "Then I saw that wisdom excelleth folly as light excelleth darkness."[8] This means that just as light has a superiority, power and dominion over darkness, so that a little physical light banishes a great deal of darkness, which is therewith inevitably superseded, as a matter of course and necessity, so is much foolishness of the kelipah and sitra achra (as, indeed, our Sages say, "A man does not sin unless a spirit of folly enters into him"[9]) inevitably driven away by the wisdom that is in the divine soul in the brain, whose desire is to rule alone in the "city" and to pervade the whole body, in the manner already

---

5. The evil nature is then temporarily repressed, but not sublimated.

6. Cf. Zohar III, p. 224a.

7. The doctrine of the inherent supremacy of "intellect over emotion" is one of the basic, though not original, tenets of Chabad. Cf. Maimonides, Guide III, 8.

8. Ecclesiastes 2:13.

9. Sotah 3a.

mentioned,[10] by means of her three garments, namely, thought, speech and act of the 613 commandments of the Torah, as explained earlier.

[*Tanya*, ch. 12, pp. 47-49.]

MIND OVER MATTER

THEREWITH WILL BE UNDERSTOOD the commentary of our Sages[1] that "'Intermediate' people are judged by both [the good and evil natures], for it is written, 'He stands at the right hand of the poor man, to save him from them that judge his soul.'"[2]

Note that they did not say "ruled" by both, G-d forbid, because where the evil nature gains any control and dominion over the "small city," even though but temporarily, one is at such times deemed "wicked."

The evil nature [in the *benoni*], however, is no more than, for example, a magistrate or judge who gives his opinion on a point of law, yet it is not necessarily a final decision to be implemented in deed, for there is another magistrate or judge who is contesting this opinion. It is therefore necessary to arbitrate between the two, and the final verdict rests with the arbitrator.

Similarly, the evil nature states its opinion in the left part of the heart,[3] which thence ascends to the brain for contemplation. Immediately it is challenged by the second judge, the divine soul in the brain[4] extending into the right part of the heart, the abode of the good nature. The final verdict comes from the arbitrator— the Holy One, blessed be He, Who comes to the aid of the good nature, as our Sages said, "If the Almighty did not help him, he could not overcome his evil inclination."[5] The help comes by means of the glow radiated by the Divine light, which illuminates

10. *Supra*, ch. 9.

1. *Brachot* 61b.
2. "Them that judge"—in the plural, allegorically interpreted to refer to the two impulses which motivate man's actions.
3. The "seat" of the passions. Cf. supra, ch. 9.
4. The intellect is the forte of the divine soul. Ibid.
5. *Kiddushin* 30b.

the divine soul that it may gain the upper hand and mastery over the folly of the fool and evil nature, in the manner of the excellence of light over darkness, as stated above.[6]

[*Tanya*, ch. 13, pp. 53.]

THE RANK OF *BENONI* IS ONE that is attainable by every man, and each person should strive after it. Every person can at any time or hour be an "intermediate," because the "intermediate" man does not revile evil[1]—for that is a feeling entrusted to the heart, and not all times are alike.[2] [His task is] only to "turn away from evil and do good," in actual practice—in deed, speech or thought, wherein the choice, ability and freedom are given to every man that he may act, speak and think even what is contrary to the desire of his heart and diametrically opposed to it.[3] Even when the heart craves and desires a material pleasure, whether permitted or, G-d forbid, prohibited, he can steel himself and divert his attention from it altogether, declaring to himself, "I will not be wicked even for a moment, because I will not be parted and separated, Heaven forefend! from the One G-d under any circumstances, being mindful of the admonition, 'Your iniquities interpose between you and G-d.'[4] Nay, my real desire is to unite my *nefesh*, *ruach* and *neshamah* with Him, through investing them in His blessed three garments, namely, in action, speech and thought dedicated to G-d, His Torah and His commandments, by virtue of the love of G-d that is hidden in my heart, as in the heart of all Jews, who are called 'lovers of Thy Name.'[5] Even the most worthless of worthless is capable of sacrificing himself for the sanctity of G-d; surely, I am not inferior to him. It is only that a spirit of folly has overcome him, and he imagines that committing a sin will not affect his Jewishness and his soul will not be severed thereby from the G-d of Israel, forgetting also about his love of G-d which is hidden in his heart. But as for me, I have no

---

6. Ch. 12.

1. Cf. supra, chaps. 11 and 12.
2. Prayer-time, for instance, is more propitious, as mentioned in chap. 12.
3. Note that "thought" is also included in the ability of self-control.
4. Isaiah 59:2.
5. Psalms 5:21.

desire to be such a fool as he to deny the truth!"

[*Tanya*, ch. 14, pp. 59.]

TRUE SERVICE

IN THE CATEGORY OF *BENONI* there are also to be found two gradations, to wit, "one who is serving G-d" and "one who serves Him not."[1] Yet the latter is not wicked, for never in his life did he commit even a minor transgression and, moreover, he fulfilled all the commandments which were possible for him to fulfill, including the study of the Torah which balances everything else, his mouth never ceasing from study. The reason he is referred to as "one who serves Him not" is that he does not wage any battle against his [evil] disposition in order to vanquish it by means of the Divine light that irradiates the divine soul, whose abode is in the brain which predominates over the heart, as explained above;[2] for his disposition does not confront him at all in an attempt to distract him from study and prayer, and he is consequently never obliged to wage war against it. Thus, for example, is the case of one who is by nature an assiduous student because he is organically so disposed, and is likewise free from conflict with regard to sexual desire by reason of his frigid nature, and similarly with the other mundane pleasures wherein he naturally lacks any feeling of enjoyment. Hence he does not need to concentrate so much on the greatness of G-d to consciously create a spirit of knowledge and fear of G-d in his mind, in order to guard himself against violation of the prohibitive commandments; or to arouse the love of G-d in his heart to induce his attachment to Him through the fulfillment of the [positive] commandments and the study of the Torah which balances everything else. For him suffices the hidden love that is in the heart of all Jews, who are called "the lovers of His name."[3] Therefore he is in no wise called "one who is serving," inasmuch as this latent love is not of his

---

1. In the sense that he requires little or no effort, by virtue of his natural disposition, as subsequently explained.
2. Ch. 12.
3. Psalms 69:37.

making or accomplishment by any means, but it is our inheritance that has come down from the Patriarchs to the whole community of Israel, as will be discussed further.[4]

So, too, is one who, although by nature not an assiduous student, has yet accustomed himself to study with great diligence, so that the habit has become second nature with him; for him, too, suffices the innate love, unless he wishes to study more than his wont.... For in order to change his habitual nature, he must arouse the love of G-d by means of meditation in his mind on the greatness of G-d, in order to gain mastery over the nature that is in the left part [of the heart] which is full of blood of the animal soul originating in the *kelipah*, whence comes his nature. This is a perfect service for a *benoni*. Or, he must awaken the hidden love in his heart to control,[5] through it, the nature that is in the left part, for this, too, is called service—the waging of war against his nature and inclination, by means of exciting the love that is hidden in his heart. However, if he wages no war at all, the said love in itself can in no way be credited to his service.

[*Tanya*, ch. 15, pp. 63-67.]

MEDITATION

THIS, THEN, IS THE IMPORTANT PRINCIPLE regarding the Divine Service for the *benoni*: The essential thing is to govern and rule the nature that is in the left ventricle [of the heart] by means of the Divine light that irradiates the divine soul in the mind.[1] That is to say, to rule the heart by means of meditation in the mind on the greatness of the blessed *En Sof*, whereby his understanding will beget a spirit of knowledge and fear of the Lord in his mind, to make him turn away from the evil condemned by the Torah, or by the Rabbis, even from a minor Rabbinic prohibition, Heaven forbid; and [at the same time arousing] the love of G-d in his heart, in the right part, with a fervor and desire to cleave

---

4. Chaps. 18, 19, and 44.
5. In this case—without changing his nature; only keeping it in check.

1. Cf. *supra*, ch. 13.

to Him through the fulfillment of the precepts of the Torah and of the Rabbis, and through the study of the Torah which is equivalent to them all.

Furthermore, one must know an additional important principle in the service of the "intermediates." This is that even if the capacity of one's intellect and the spirit of one's understanding do not attain to the level of producing a revealed love of G-d in one's heart, to make it glow like burning coals with a great desire and yearning and heartfelt passion to cleave unto Him, but the love is hidden in one's brain and in the recesses of one's heart.... Consequently, when [the *benoni*] ponders this subject in the recesses of his heart's and mind's understanding, with a unanimity of mouth and heart, in that he upholds by word of mouth that which has been resolved in the understanding of his heart and mind, namely, to direct his desire towards the Divine Torah, meditating on it day and night in oral study, while his hands and other bodily organs carry out the commandments, in accordance with the resolution of his heart's and mind's understanding, then this understanding is clothed in the act, speech and thought of the Torah and its commandments, providing for them, as it were, intelligence, vitality and "wings" wherewith to soar on high.

[*Tanya*, ch. 16, pp. 67-69.]

...AND ACTION

WITH THE ABOVE IN MIND, one can understand the Scriptural text, "But the thing is very nigh unto thee, in thy mouth and in thy heart, that thou mayest *do it*."[1]

At first glance, the statement that "the thing is very nigh unto thee...in thy heart" seems to be contrary to our experience (yet the Torah is eternal).[2] For it is not a "very nigh thing" to change one's heart from mundane desires to a sincere love of G-d. Indeed, it is stated in the Gemara, "Is fear [of Heaven] a

---

1. Deuteronomy 30:14.

2. Hence it could not refer to the time of Moses only, but must hold good for our time as well.

small thing?"[3] How much more so—love. Moreover, the Rabbis also said, that only *tzaddikim* have control over their hearts.[4]

But the words "that thou mayest do it" refer to a love which merely leads to the performance of the commandments, this being the hidden desire of the heart (רעותא דלבא), even if it does not glow openly like flaming coals. This thing is very near, and it is easy for any person who has brains in his head, for his brain is under his control, and he is able to concentrate it on anything he wishes. If, then, he will contemplate with it on the greatness of the blessed *En Sof*, he will inevitably generate in his mind, at least, the love of G-d to cleave unto Him through the perform-ance of His commandments and Torah. And this constitutes the whole [purpose of] man, for it is written, "This day to do them"[5]—"this day" referring specifically to the world of [physical] action,[6] while "tomorrow" [i.e., in afterlife] is the time of reward, as is explained elsewhere.

[*Tanya*, ch. 17, pp. 71-73.]

SELF-SACRIFICE

IT SHOULD BE RECOGNIZED with certainty that even the person whose understanding in the knowledge of G-d is limited, and who has no heart to comprehend the greatness of the blessed *En Sof*, to produce therefrom awe and love [of G-d] even in his mind and understanding alone[1]—nevertheless it is a "very nigh thing" for him to observe and practise all the commandments of the Torah and the "study of the Torah which counterbalances them all," in his very mouth and heart, from the depths of his heart, in true sincerity, with fear and love; namely, the hidden love in the heart of all Jews which is an inheritance to us from our Patriarchs.... Therefore even the most worthless of worthless and

---

3. *Brachot* 33b; *Megillah* 25a.
4. *Bereshit Rabbah* 34:11, 67:7.
5. Deuteronomy 7:11.
6. *Eruvin* 22a.

1. I.e. without emotional sway.

the transgressors of the Israelites, in the majority of cases sacrifice their lives for the sanctity of G-d's Name and suffer harsh torture rather than deny the one G-d, although they be boors and illiterate and ignorant of G-d's greatness. [For] whatever little knowledge they do possess, they do not delve therein at all, [and so] they do not give up their lives by reason of any knowledge and contemplation of G-d. Rather [do they suffer martyrdom] without any knowledge and reflection, but as if it were absolutely impossible to renounce the one G-d; and without any reason or hesitation whatever. This is because the one G-d illuminates and animates the entire *nefesh*, through being clothed in its faculty of *chochmah*, which is beyond any graspable and understood knowledge or intelligence.

[*Tanya*, ch. 18, pp. 75-77.]

TO ELUCIDATE IT STILL FURTHER, it is necessary to clarify the meaning of the verse, "The candle of G-d is the soul (*neshamah*) of man."[1] What it means is that the souls of Jews, who are called "man,"[2] are, by way of illustration, like the flame of the candle, whose nature it is always to scintillate upwards, for the flame of the fire intrinsically seeks to be parted from the wick in order to unite with its source above, in the universal element of fire which is in the sublunar sphere, as is explained in *Etz Chaim*. And although it would thereby be extinguished and emit no light at all below, and even above, in its source, its light would be nullified, nevertheless this is what it seeks in accordance with its nature.

In like manner does the *neshamah* of man, including the quality of *ruach* and *nefesh*, naturally desire and yearn to separate itself and depart from the body in order to unify with its origin and source in G-d, the fountain-head of all life, blessed be He, though thereby it would become null and void, completely losing its entity therein, with nothing remaining of its former essence and being.[3] Nevertheless, this is its will and desire by its nature.

---

1. Proverbs 20:27.
2. *Yevamot* 61a.
3. This passage does not mean extinction of the soul; only its cessation as a *distinct entity*.

"Nature" is a loan-word for anything that is not in the realm of reason and comprehension. In our case, too, the inference is that this will and desire of the soul are not within the realm of reason, knowledge and intelligence; for this nature stems from the faculty of *chochmah* found in the soul, wherein abides the light of the blessed *En Sof*.... For this reason, this love of the divine soul, whose desire and wish is to unite with G-d, the blessed fountain-head of all life, is called "hidden love," for it is hidden and veiled, in the case of the transgressors of Israel, in the sackcloth of the *kelipah*, whence there enters into them a spirit of folly to sin, as the Rabbis have said, "A person does not sin unless the spirit of folly has entered into him."[4]

However, this exile of the faculty of *chochmah* refers only to that aspect of it which is diffused throughout the *nefesh* and animates it. Yet the root and core of this faculty of the divine soul remains in the brain and does not clothe itself in the sackcloth of the *kelipah* in the left part of the heart, in veritable exile, but it is, as it were, dormant in the case of the wicked, not exercising its influence in them so long as their knowledge and understanding are preoccupied with mundane pleasures. Nevertheless, when they are confronted with a test in a matter of faith, which transcends knowledge, touching the very soul and the faculty of *chochmah* within it, at such time it is aroused from its sleep and it exerts its influence by virtue of the Divine force that is clothed in it, as is written, "Then the Lord awaked as one out of sleep."[5] [On such occasion the sinner is inspired] to withstand the test of faith in G-d, without any reasoning, or knowledge, or intelligence that may be comprehended by him, and to prevail over the *kelipah* and temptations of this world, whether permitted or prohibited, to which he had been accustomed—even to despise them, and to choose G-d as his portion and lot, yielding to Him his soul [to suffer martyrdom] in order to sanctify His Name. For, even though the *kelipot* had prevailed over him all his life and he was impotent against them, as the Rabbis have said that "the wicked are under the control of their heart,"[6] yet when he faces a

---

4. *Sotah* 3a.
5. Psalms 78:65.
6. *Bereshit Rabbah* 34:11.

test challenging his faith in the one G-d, [a faith] which has its roots in the uppermost heights of holiness, namely, the faculty of *chochmah* of the divine soul, in which is clothed the light of the blessed *En Sof*, then all the *kelipot* are made null and void, and they vanish, as though they had never been, in the presence of the Lord.

[*Tanya*, ch. 19, pp. 77-81.]

THE UNITY OF G-D

WE MUST BRIEFLY REFER TO THE SUBJECT and essence of the Unity of the Holy One, blessed be He, Who is called One and Unique, and "all believe that He is All Alone,"[1] exactly as He was before the world was created, when there was naught beside Him, as is written, "Thou wast the same ere the world was created; Thou hast been the same since the world hath been created,"[2] etc. This means: exactly the same without any change, as it is written, "For I, the Lord, have not changed,"[3] inasmuch as this world and likewise all supernal worlds do not effect any change in His blessed Unity, by their having been created *ex nihilo*. For just as He was All Alone, Single and Unique, before they were created, so is He One and Alone, Single and Unique after they were created, since, beside Him, everything is as nothing, verily as null and void. For the coming into being of all the upper and nether worlds out of non-being, and their life and existence sustaining them from reverting to non-existence and nought, as was before, is nothing else but the word of G-d and the breath of His blessed mouth[4] that is clothed in them.

To illustrate from the soul of a human being:

When a man utters a word, this utterance in itself is as absolutely nothing even when compared only with his general "articulate soul," which is the so-called middle "garment,"[5] name-

---

1. Liturgy of New Year's Day and Day of Atonement.
2. Liturgy, daily Morning Service.
3. Malachi 3:6.
4. See Psalms 33:6.
5. Of the three garments: thought, *speech* and act.

ly, its faculty of speech, which can produce speech without limit or end;[6] all the more when it is compared with its so-called innermost "garment," to wit, its faculty of thought, which is the source of speech and its life-force; not to mention when it is compared with the essence and entity of the soul, these being its ten attributes mentioned above,[7] viz. *chochmah, binah, da'at* (ChaBaD), etc., from which are derived the "letters" of thought that are clothed in the speech when it is uttered. For thought can as much be defined in terms of "letters" as speech, except that in the former they are more spiritual and refined. But the ten attributes—ChaBaD, etc.—are the root and source of thought, and, prior to their being clothed in the garment of thought, still lack the element of "letters." For example, when a man suddenly becomes conscious of a certain love or desire in his heart, before it has risen from the heart to the brain to think and meditate about it, it has not yet acquired the element of "letters"; it is only a simple desire and longing in the heart for the object of his affection. All the more so before he began to feel in his heart a craving and desire for that thing, and it is as yet confined within the realm of his wisdom, intellect and knowledge, that is, the thing is known to him to be desirable and gratifying, something good and pleasant to attain and to cling to, as, for instance, to learn some wisdom or to eat some delicious food. Only after the desire and craving have already found their way into the heart, through the stimulus of his wisdom, intellect and knowledge, and thence ascended once more back to the brain, to think and meditate on how to translate his craving from the potential into the practical, with a view to actually obtaining that food or acquiring that wisdom—it is here that the so-called "letters" are born in his mind, such "letters" corresponding to the language of each nation, employing them in speech and thought about all things in the world.[8]

[*Tanya*, ch. 20, pp. 83-87.]

HOWEVER, "THE NATURE OF THE DIVINE ORDER is not like that of

---

6. Physical incapacity (or death) does not limit the soul's potential capacity for speech, which is intrinsic to it.

7. Ch. 3.

8. Continued in next chapter.

a creature of flesh and blood."[1] When a man utters a word, the breath emitted in speaking is something that can be sensed and perceived as a thing apart, separated from its source, namely, the ten faculties of the soul itself. But with the Holy One, blessed be He, His speech is not, Heaven forfend, separated from His blessed Self, for there is nothing outside of Him, and there is no place devoid of Him.[2] Therefore, His blessed speech is not like our speech, G-d forbid, (just as His thought is not like our thought, as it written, "For My thoughts are not like your thoughts,"[3] and "So My ways are higher than your ways,"[4] etc.). His blessed speech is called "speech" only by way of an anthropomorphic illustration, in the sense that, as in the case of man below, whose speech reveals to his audience what was hidden and concealed in his thoughts, so, too, is it On High with the blessed *En Sof*, Whose emitted light and life-force—as it emerges from Him, from concealment into revelation, to create worlds and to sustain them—is called "speech." These [emanations] are indeed, the ten fiats by which the world was created;[5] likewise also the remainder of the Torah, Prophets and Hagiographa, which the prophets conceived in their prophetic vision.

Yet His so-called speech and thought are united with Him in absolute union as, for example, a person's speech and thought whilst they are still *in potentia* in his wisdom and intellect, or in a desire and craving that are still in the heart prior to rising from the heart to the brain, where by cogitation they are formulated into the so-called "letters"; for at that time the "letters" of thought and speech which evolve from that longing or desire, were still *in potentia* in the heart, where they were absolutely fused with their root, namely, the wisdom and intellect in the brain, and the longing and desire in the heart.

Verily so, by way of example, are the "speech" and "thought" of the Holy One, blessed be He, absolutely united with His blessed essence and being, even after His blessed "speech" has

---

1. *Brachot* 40a.
2. *Tikkunei Zohar, Tikkun* 57, p. 91b.
3. Isaiah 55:8.
4. Ibid., v. 9.
5. *Avot* 5:1.

already become materialized in the creation of the worlds, just as it was united with Him ere the worlds were created. There is thus no manner of change in His blessed Self, but only for the created beings which receive their life-force from His blessed "word," as it were, in its revealed state at the creation of the worlds, in which it is clothed, giving them life through a process of gradual descent from cause to effect and a downward gradation, by means of numerous and various contractions,[6] until the created beings can receive their life and existence from it, without losing their entity. These "contractions" are all in the nature of "veiling of the Countenance," to obscure and conceal the light and life-force that are derived from His blessed "word," so that it shall not reveal itself in a greater radiance than the lower worlds are capable of receiving. Hence it seems to them as if the light and life-force of the Omnipresent, blessed be He, which is clothed in them, were something apart from His blessed Self, and it only issues from Him, just as the speech of a human being [issues] from his soul. Yet, in regard to the Holy One, blessed be He, no concealment or delitescence hides or obscures anything from Him, to Whom darkness is like light, as is written, "Yea, the darkness obscureth not from Thee,"[7] etc. For all the "contractions" and "garments" are not things distinct from Him, Heaven forfend, but "like the snail, whose garment is part of his body,"[8] and as is written, "The Lord, He is G-d,"[9] as is explained elsewhere.[10] Therefore, in His Presence all else is of no account whatever.

[*Tanya,* ch. 21.]

SERVICE WITH JOY

TRULY THIS SHOULD BE MADE KNOWN as a cardinal principle, that

---

6. The process of *tzimtzum.*
7. Psalms 139:12.
8. *Bereshit Rabbah* 21.
9. Deuteronomy 4:35.
10. The Tetragrammaton (YHVH, usually translated "the L-rd") is conceived in Kabbalah as the transcendent creative Divine force, while *Elohim* ("G-d")—the immanent Divine force concealed in nature. Cf. *Shaar Hayichud v'haEmunah,* chap. 6. The equation emphasizes the absolute Unity of the Creator.

as with a victory over a physical obstacle, such as in the case of two individuals who are wrestling with each other, each striving to throw the other—if one is lazy and sluggish he will easily be defeated and thrown, even though he be stronger than the other, exactly so is it in the conquest of one's evil nature; it is impossible to conquer it with laziness and heaviness, which originate in sadness and in a heart that is dulled like a stone, but rather with alacrity which derives from joy and from a heart that is free and cleansed from any trace of worry and sadness in the world.

As for what is written, "In all sadness there would be profit,"[1] which means that some profit and advantage would be derived from it, the phrase, on the contrary, indicates that sadness in itself has no virtue, except that some profit is derived and experienced from it, namely, the true joy in the L-rd G-d which follows at propitious moments from genuine anguish over one's sins, with bitterness of soul and a broken heart. For thereby the spirit of impurity and of the *sitra achra* is broken, as also the iron wall that separates him from his Father in Heaven, as is commented in the *Zohar* on the verse, "A broken and a contrite heart, O G-d, Thou wilt not despise;"[2] then will be fulfilled in him the preceding verses: "Make me hear joy and gladness...Restore unto me the joy of Thy salvation, and uphold me with Thy generous spirit."[3]... The following is sound counsel as to how to cleanse one's heart of all sadness and of every trace of worry about mundane matters, even about "children, health and sustenance." Everyone is familiar with the statement of the Rabbis that "just as one must recite a blessing for the good, [one must also recite a blessing for misfortune].[4] In the Gemara it is explained that one should accept [misfortune] with joy, like the joy of a visible and obvious benefit, "for this is also for the good," except that it is not apparent and visible to mortal eyes, because it stems from the "hidden world" which is higher than the "revealed world."... Hence the meaning of the verse, "Happy is the man whom Thou, O G-d, chasteneth."[5]

1. Proverbs 14:23.
2. Psalms 51:19.
3. Ibid., vs. 10, 14.
4. *Brachot*, chap. 9, Mishnah 5.
5. Psalms 94:12.

Therefore, the Rabbis, of blessed memory, commented[6] that it is to those who rejoice in their afflictions that the verse refers: "But they that love Him shall be as the sun going forth in its might."[7] For this is the joy of desiring the nearness of G-d more than anything in the life of this world, as is written, "Because Thy lovingkindness is better than life,"[8] etc.... Therefore, [the man who accepts affliction with joy], merits [to see] the "sun going forth in its might"—in the world to come, i.e. the sun emerging from its sheath in which it is enclosed in this world.[9] But in the world to come it will appear out of its covering, meaning that then the "hidden world" will be revealed and will shine and send forth light in a great and intense revelation to those who had taken refuge in Him....

As for the sadness which is connected with heavenly[10] matters, one must seek ways and means of freeing oneself from it, to say nothing of the time of Divine Service, when one must serve G-d with gladness and a joyful heart....

Thus, whether the melancholy encroaches on him during Divine Service, in study or prayer, or not during Divine Service, he should tell himself that now is not the time for genuine anxiety, not even for worry over serious transgressions, G-d forbid. For, for this, one needs appointed times and a propitious occasion, with calmness of mind to reflect on the greatness of G-d, against Whom one has sinned, so that thereby one's heart may truly be rent with sincere contrition. It is explained elsewhere when this time should be, and it is there explained also that as soon as his heart has been broken during these specific occasions, he should forthwith completely remove the sorrow from his heart and believe with a perfect faith that G-d has removed his sin in His abundant forgiveness. This is the true joy in G-d which comes after the remorse, as mentioned above.

[*Tanya*, ch. 26, pp. 111-115.]

---

6. *Yoma* 23a.
7. Judges 5:31.
8. Psalms 63:4.
9. Cf. *Nedarim* 8b.
10. I.e. failure in matters of the spirit.

SHOULD THE SADNESS, HOWEVER, not come from worry over sins, but from evil thoughts and desires that enter his mind—if they enter not during Divine Service but whilst he is occupied with his own affairs and with mundane matters and the like, he should, on the contrary, be happy in his portion in that, though they enter his mind, he averts his mind from them in order to fulfill the injunction, "That ye seek not after your own heart and your own eyes, after which ye go astray."[1] The verse does not speak of the righteous, to refer to them as "going astray," G-d forbid, but of "Intermediates" (benonim) like him, in whose mind do enter erotic thoughts whether of an innocent nature, etc.;[2] when he averts his mind from them, he is fulfilling this injunction. Indeed, the Rabbis, of blessed memory, have said, "He who has passively abstained from committing a sin, receives a reward as though he had performed a precept."[3]

Consequently, he should rejoice at his compliance with the injunction as when performing an actual positive precept....

Therefore, no person should feel depressed, nor should his heart become exceedingly troubled, even though he be engaged all his days in this conflict, for perhaps because of this was he created and this is his service—constantly to subjugate the sitra achra.

[Tanya, ch. 27, pp. 115-117.]

NEVERTHELESS HE MUST NOT BE DOWNCAST at heart and feel dejected and despicable during Divine Service, which should be with great joy. On the contrary, he should draw fresh strength and intensify [his] effort with all his power to concentrate on the prayer with increased joy and gladness, in the realization that the foreign thought that had invaded his heart comes from the kelipah in the left part, which, in the case of the benoni, wages war with the divine soul within him. For it is known that the way of combatants, as of wrestlers, is that when one is gaining the upper hand the other likewise strives to prevail with all the resources of his strength. Therefore, when the divine soul exerts itself and summons its strength for prayer, the kelipah also gathers strength

---

1. Numbers 15:39.
2. "...or otherwise."
3. Kiddushin 39b.

146

at such time to confuse her and topple her by means of a foreign thought of its own. This refutes the error commonly held by people, who mistakenly deduce from the occurrence of the foreign thought that this proves their prayer to be worthless, for if one prayed as is fitting and proper no foreign thoughts would have occurred to him. What they say would be true if there were only one single soul, the same that prays as well as thinks and fancies the foreign thoughts.

The real truth, however, is that there are two souls, waging war one against the other in the person's mind, each one wishing and desiring to rule over him and pervade his mind exclusively. Thus all thoughts of Torah and the fear of Heaven come from the divine soul, while all mundane matters come from the animal soul, except that the divine soul is clothed in it. This is like the example of a person praying with devotion, while facing him there stands a wicked heathen who chats and speaks to him in order to confuse him. Surely the thing to do in such a case would be not to answer him good or evil, but rather to pretend to be deaf without hearing, and to comply with the verse, "Answer not a fool according to his folly, lest thou also be like unto him."[1] Similarly, he must answer nothing, nor engage in any argument and counter-argument with the foreign thought, for he who wrestles with a filthy person is bound to become soiled himself. Rather should he adopt an attitude as if he neither knows nor hears the thoughts that have befallen him; he must remove them from his mind and strengthen still more the power of his concentration. However, if he finds it hard to dismiss them from his mind, because they distract his mind with great intensity, then he should humble his spirit before G-d and supplicate Him in his thought to have compassion upon him in His abundant mercies, as a father who takes pity on his children; so may the L-rd have pity on his soul which is derived from Him Who is blessed, and deliver it from the "turbulent waters;"[2] for His sake He will do it, for verily "His people is a part of the Lord."[3]

[Tanya, ch. 28, pp. 121-123.]

---

1. Proverbs 26:4.
2. Allusion to Psalms 124:5.
3. Deuteronomy 32:9. Thus, by helping the divine soul, G-d helps Himself, as it were.

Dimensions of Service

IT IS INDEED A GREAT AND FIERCE STRUGGLE to break one's passion, which burns like a fiery flame, through fear of G-d; it is like an actual test. Therefore, each person according to his place and rank in the service of G-d must weigh and examine his position as to whether he is serving G-d in a manner commensurate with the dimensions of such a fierce battle and test—in the realm of "do good,"[1] as, for example, in the service of prayer with *kavanah* (devotion), pouring out his soul before G-d with his entire strength, to the point of exhaustion of the soul,[2] while waging war against his body and animal soul within it which impede his devotion, a strenuous war to beat and grind them like dust, each day before the morning and evening prayers.

So, too, with the other commandments, especially in matters involving money, as the service of charity (*tzedakah*) and similar.

Even in the category of "turn away from evil" every intelligent person can discover within himself that he does not turn aside from evil completely and in every respect where a hard battle at a level such as described above is called for, or even on a lesser level than the aforementioned: for example, to stop in the middle of a pleasant gossip, or in the middle of a tale discrediting his fellow, even though it be a very small slur, and even though it be true, and even when the purpose is to exonerate oneself....

The same applies to very many similar things which occur frequently, especially with regard to sanctifying oneself in permissible things, an enactment based on the Biblical text, "Ye shall be holy,"[3] etc., and "Sanctify yourselves, therefore,"[4] etc. Moreover, "Rabbinic enactments are even stricter than Biblical enactments,"[5] and so forth. But all these and similar ones are of the sins which a person tramples under-foot and has come to regard as

---

1. Psalms 34.15. That of "turn away from evil" will follow later.
2. *Sifre* on Deuteronomy 6:5—עד מיצוי הנפש—literally, to the extent of "wringing out" the soul.
3. Leviticus 19:2.
4. Ibid. 20:7.
5. *Sanhedrin*, 11:3; *Brachot* 3b; *Avodah Zara* 41a; *Rosh Hashanah* 19a; *Yevamot* 85b.

permissible in consequence of repeated transgression, etc.[6]

[*Tanya,* ch. 30, pp. 135-137.]

[OCCASIONALLY], THE METHOD OF SUBDUING the *sitra achra* is on the latter's own ground, as the Rabbis of blessed memory have said, "From the forest itself is taken the axe wherewith to fell it,"[1] and "he met his equal."[2] With regard to this it is written, "In all sadness there is profit,"[3] the profit being the joy that follows the sadness, as will be explained later.

In truth, however, a contrite heart and the bitterness[4] of the soul because of its remoteness from the light of the Divine countenance and its being clothed in the *sitra achra*—are not called *atzvut* (dejection) in the sacred tongue, for *atzvut* implies that the heart is dull like a stone and is devoid of vitality. But in the case of *merirut* (bitterness) and a broken heart, the contrary is surely true—there is vitality in the heart fermenting agitation and bitterness, except that this vitality stems from the attribute of the holy *gevurot* (severity), whereas joy comes from the attribute of *chasadim* (kindness), for the heart is comprised of them both.

[*Tanya,* ch. 31, pp. 139.]

AHAVAT YISRAEL

A DIRECT AND EASY WAY TO ATTAIN the fulfillment of the commandment "Thou shalt love thy fellow as thyself"[1] toward every soul of Israel, both great and small —

...The soul and spirit—who can know their greatness and excellence in their root and source in the living G-d? being,

---

6. *Avodah Zara* 18a.

1. *Sanhedrin* 39b.
2. *Shabbat* 121b.
3. Proverbs 14:23.
4. The author makes a distinction between עצבות ("sadness," bordering on depression or melancholy) and מרירות ("bitterness").

1. Leviticus 19:18.

moreover, all of a kind and all having one Father. Therefore, all Israelites are called real brothers by virtue of the source of their souls in the one G-d; only the bodies are separated. Hence in the case of those who give major consideration to their body while regarding their soul as of secondary importance, there can be no true love and brotherhood among them, but only [a love] which is dependent on a [transitory] thing.[2]

This is what Hillel the Elder meant when he said in regard to the fulfillment of this commandment, "This is the whole Torah, whilst the rest is but commentary,"[3] etc. For the basis and root of the entire Torah is to raise and exalt the soul high above the body, reaching unto the Source and Root of all the worlds, and also to bring down the blessed light of the *En Sof* upon the community of Israel, as will be explained later,[4] i.e. into the fountain-head of the souls of all Israel, to become "one into One."[5] This is impossible if there is G-d forbid, disunity among the souls, for the Holy One, blessed be He, does not dwell in an imperfect place,[6] as we pray: "Bless us, O our Father, all of us together, with the light of Thy countenance,"[7] as has been explained at great length elsewhere.

[*Tanya*, ch. 32, pp. 145.]

TORAH AND MITZVOT

THIS, ALSO, WILL BE THE TRUE JOY OF THE SOUL, especially when one recognizes, at appropriate times, that one needs to purify and illuminate one's soul with gladness of the heart. Let him then concentrate his mind and envisage in his intelligence and understanding the subject of His blessed true Unity....

When one will deeply contemplate this, his heart will be gladdened and his soul will rejoice even with joy and singing,

2. *Avot* 5:16.
3. *Shabbat* 31a.
4. Ch. 41.
5. *Zohar* II, 135a.
6. *Zohar* I, 216b.
7. Liturgy, *Amidah*.

with all heart and soul and might, in [the intensity of] this faith which is tremendous, since this is the [experience of the] very proximity of G-d, and it is the whole [purpose] of man and the goal of his creation, as well as of the creation of all the worlds, both upper and lower, that He may have an abode here below, as will later be explained at length.[1]

Behold, how great is the joy of a common and lowly man when he is brought near to a king of flesh and blood, who accepts his hospitality and lodges under his roof! How infinitely more so is the [joy in the] abiding nearness of the Supreme King of kings, the Holy One, blessed be He.

[*Tanya*, ch. 33, pp. 147-149.]

THE *NESHAMAH* OF A PERSON—even if he be a perfect *tzaddik* serving G-d with fear and love of delights[1]—does not, nevertheless, completely dissolve itself out of existence, so as to be truly nullified and absorbed into the light of G-d to the extent of becoming one and the same absolutely, but the person remains an entity apart, one who fears G-d and loves Him. It is different, however, with the commandments and good deeds, which are His blessed will. His blessed will is the source of life for all the worlds and creatures, flowing down to them through many contractions (*tzimtzumim*) and the concealment of the countenance of the Supreme Will (*Ratzon Elyon*), blessed be He, and the recession of the levels, until it was made possible for creatures to come into being *ex nihilo*, separate beings that should not lose their identity, as discussed above.[2]

The commandments, however, are different in that they are the inwardness of His blessed will, without any concealment of the Countenance whatever; the vitality that is in them [therefore] is in no way a separate, independent thing, but is united and absorbed in His blessed will, and they become truly one with a perfect union....

Therefore, when a person occupies himself in the Torah, his

---

1. Explained at length in chaps. 20 and 21.

1. Cf. *supra*, chs. 9, 14.
2. Chs. 10, 21, 22.

neshamah, which is his divine soul, with her two innermost garments only, namely the power of speech and thought, are absorbed in the Divine light of the blessed *En Sof*, and are united with it in a perfect union. This constitutes the resting of the *Shechinah* on his divine soul, as the Rabbis stated, "Even if one person sedulously occupies himself with the Torah, the *Shechinah* is with him."[3]

However, in order to draw the light and effulgence of the *Shechinah* also over his body and animal soul, i.e. on the vital spirit clothed in the physical body, he needs to fulfill the practical commandments which are performed by the body itself. For then the very energy of the body itself which is engaged in this action is absorbed in the Divine light and in His will, and is united with Him in a perfect union. This is the third garment of the divine soul. Thereby also the energy of the vital spirit in the physical body, originating in the *kelipat nogah*, is transformed from evil to good, and is actually absorbed into holiness like the divine soul itself, since it is this [animal soul] that carries out and performs the act of the commandment, because without it the divine soul could not have been acting through the body at all, for it is spiritual whilst the body is material and coarse. The intermediary linking them is the vital animal soul, which is clothed in the human blood, in the heart and in all the body.

[*Tanya*, ch. 35, pp. 157-161.]

MESSIANIC ERA AND RESURRECTION

IT IS WELL KNOWN THAT THE MESSIANIC ERA, and especially the time of the Resurrection of the Dead, is the fulfillment and culmination of the creation of the world, for which purpose it was originally created.

Something of this revelation has already been experienced on earth, at the time of the Giving of the Torah, as is written, "Unto thee it was showed, that thou mightest know that the L-rd He is G-d; there is naught else beside Him"[1]—"it was

---

3. *Brachot* 6a.

1. Deuteronomy 4:35.

showed" verily with physical vision, as is written, "And all the people *saw* the thunderings"[2]—"they saw what is [normally] heard."[3]... This was so because of the revelation of His blessed will in the Decalogue constituting the epitome of the whole Torah,[4] which is the inwardness of His blessed will and wisdom, wherein there is no concealment of the Countenance at all, as is written, "For in the light of Thy Countenance hast Thou given us the Law of life."[5] Therefore they [the Israelites at Sinai] repeatedly expired out of existence, as the Rabbis have taught that "at each [Divine] utterance their soul took flight, etc., but the Holy One, blessed be He, restored it to them with the dew wherewith He will revive the dead."[6] This is the dew of the Torah which is called "might," as the Rabbis have said, "Everyone who occupies himself with the Torah is revived by the dew of the Torah," etc.[7] Later, however, the sin [of the Golden Calf] caused both them and the world to become gross again—until "the end of days," when the dross of the body and of the world will be purified, and they will be able to apprehend the revealed Divine light which will shine forth to Israel by means of the Torah, called "might." And, as a result of the overflow of the illumination on Israel, the darkness of the gentiles will also be lit up, as is written, "And the nations shall walk by Thy light,"[8] etc., and, "O, house of Jacob, come ye, and let us walk in the light of the L-rd";[9] again, "And the glory of the L-rd shall be revealed, and all flesh shall see together."[10]...

[*Tanya*, ch. 36, pp. 163-167.]

THIS CULMINATING FULFILLMENT of the Messianic Era and of the Resurrection of the Dead, which is the revelation of the light of the blessed *En Sof* in this material world, depends on our actions

---

2. Literally: "voices." Exodus 20:15.
3. *Mechilta*, on the verse.
4. *Rashi*, Exodus 24:12; *Zohar* II, 90b.
5. Liturgy, *Amidah* Prayer.
6. *Shabbat* 88b.
7. *Ketubot* 111b.
8. Isaiah 60:3.
9. Ibid. 2:5.
10. Ibid. 40:5.

and service throughout the duration of the *galut*. For what causes the reward of a commandment is the commandment itself,[1] because by virtue of performing it the person suffuses a flood of light of the blessed *En Sof* from above downwards, to be clothed in the corporeality of the world, in something that was previously under the dominion of the *kelipat nogah*, from which it had received its vitality. These are all those things that are [ritually] clean and permissible, wherewith the precept of action is performed, viz., parchment used in the phylacteries and *mezuzah* and the scroll of the Torah,...so, too, money given to charity which had not been dishonestly acquired; and similarly with other things.

Thus, when a person performs the Divine commandment and will, by means of these ["clean" things], the vitality that is in them ascends and is dissolved and absorbed into the light of the blessed *En Sof*, which is His blessed will that is clothed in them, since therein there is no concealment of Countenance whatever, to obscure His blessed light.

In like manner, the energy of the vital animal soul which is in the organs of the body of the person performing the commandment, is also clothed in this performance, and it rises from the *kelipah* and is absorbed into the holiness of the precept, which is His blessed will, and is dissolved into the light of the blessed *En Sof*....

[*Tanya*, ch. 37, pp. 167-169.]

TZEDAKAH

IN THE LIGHT OF THE ABOVE, one can understand why our Rabbis, of blessed memory, so strongly emphasized the virtue of charity,[1] declaring that "it balances all the other commandments,"[2] and throughout the Yerushalmi Talmud it is called simply "The Commandment," for such was the usage of the language to call charity simply "The Commandment," because it is the core of the

---

1. Cf. *Avot* 4:2.

1. *Bava Batra* 9a.
2. Ibid.

precepts of action and surpasses them all. For all [precepts] are only intended to elevate the vital soul unto G-d, since it is she [the soul] that performs them and clothes itself in them, thereby being absorbed into the light of the blessed *En Sof* which is vested in them. Hence you can find no commandment in which the vital soul is clothed to the same extent as in the commandment of charity: for in all [the other] commandments only one faculty of the vital soul is embodied, and then only at the time of the performance of the precept, whilst in the case of charity, which a man gives out of the toil of his hands, surely all the strength of his vital soul is embodied in the execution of his work or occupation by which he earned the money; when he gives it for charity, his whole vital soul ascends to G-d. Even where one does not depend on his toil for a livelihood, nevertheless since with this [charity] money he could have purchased necessities of life, for his vivifying soul, hence he is giving his soul's life to G-d.

Therefore our Rabbis, of blessed memory, said that it [charity] brings the Redemption nearer.[3] For with one act of charity a person elevates a great part of the vivifying soul, of whose powers and faculties he cannot elevate in the same measure by performing several other active precepts.

As for the statement of our Rabbis that "the study of the Torah equals all other commandments combined,"[4] this is because Torah study is effected through the faculties of speech and thought, which are the innermost garments of the vivifying soul; also the essence and substance of the faculties of ChaBaD (*chochmah*, *binah*, *da'at*) of the *kelipat nogah* in the vivifying soul are integrated into holiness itself when one occupies oneself in Torah with concentration and intelligence....

[*Tanya*, ch. 37, pp. 175-177.]

TORAH STUDY AND PRACTICE

FURTHERMORE, AND THIS IS THE most important aspect of all in

---

3. Ibid., 10a.
4. *Peah* 1:1.

the pre-eminence of Torah study over all other commandments, based on the above-mentioned[6] quotation from the *Tikkunim*, that "the 248 commandments are the 248 'organs' of the King": Just as in the case of a human being, by way of example, there is no comparison or similitude between the vitality that is in his 248 organs and the vitality that is in the brain, i.e. the intellect which is subdivided into the three faculties of ChaBaD, exactly analogous, by way of example, yet removed by myriads of distinctions *ad infinitum*, is the illumination of the light of the blessed *En Sof* in the ChaBaD aspects of the wisdom of the Torah, in each man according to his intelligence and mental grasp. And although his apprehension is only in its material aspects, yet the Torah is likened to water, which descends from a high level, etc., as has been explained above.[7]

Nevertheless, the Rabbis declared, "Not learning, but doing is the essential thing."[8] It is also written, "this day to *do* them."[9] And [it has been ruled that] one should interrupt the study of the Torah in order to fulfill an active precept that cannot be performed by others.[10] For, "this is the whole man,"[11] and the purpose of his creation and his descent to this world, in order that He have an abode here below especially, to turn darkness into light, so that the glory of the L-rd shall fill all of this material world, with the emphasis on *material*, and "all flesh shall see it together," as has been discussed above.

[*Tanya*, ch. 37, pp. 177-179.]

YOKE OF HEAVENLY KINGDOM

ONE MUST, HOWEVER, CONSTANTLY bear in mind the beginning of the service and its core and root. By this is meant that, although fear is the root of "depart from evil" and love—of "do good," nev-

---

6. Ch. 23.
7. Ch.4.
8. *Avot* 1:17.
9. Deuteronomy 7:11.
10. *Moed Katan* 9b.
11. Ecclesiastes 12:13.

ertheless it is not sufficient to awaken the love alone to do good, but one must at least first arouse the innate fear which lies hidden in the heart of every Jew not to rebel against the Supreme King of kings, the Holy One, blessed be He, as has been stated above,[1] so that this [fear] shall manifest itself in his heart or, at least, his mind. This means that he should at least contemplate in his thought on the greatness of the blessed *En Sof*, and on His Kingship, which extends in all worlds, both higher and lower, and that "He fills all worlds and encompasses all worlds," as is written: "Do I not fill heaven and earth?"[2] Yet He leaves both the higher and lower [worlds] and uniquely bestows His Kingdom upon His people Israel, in general and upon him in particular, as, indeed, a man is obliged to say: "For my sake was the world created."[3] And on his part, he accepts His Kingdom upon himself, that He be King over him, to serve Him and do His will in all kinds of servile work. "And, behold, G-d stands over him,"[4] and "the whole world is full of His glory,"[5] and He looks upon him and "searches his reins and heart"[6] [to see] if he is serving Him as is fitting. Therefore he must serve in His presence with awe and fear like one standing before the king.

One must meditate profoundly and at length on this thought according to the capacity of apprehension of his brain and thought, and for as long a time as he can spare, before he occupies himself with Torah or a commandment, such as prior to putting on his *tallit* or phylacteries. He should also reflect how the light of the blessed *En Sof*, which encompasses all worlds and pervades all worlds, which is identical with the Higher Will, is clothed in the letters and wisdom of the Torah and in the *tzitzit* (Fringes) and the phylacteries, and through his study or donning these latter he draws over himself His blessed light, that is, over "the portion of G-dliness from above" which is within his body,[7] that it may be absorbed and nullified in His blessed light.

1. Ch. 4; see also end of chs. 19, 38.
2. Jeremiah 23:24.
3. *Sanhedrin* 4:5.
4. Allusion to Genesis 28:13.
5. Isaiah 6:3.
6. Jeremiah 11:20.
7. See beg. ch. 2.

Specifically, in the case of the phylacteries, [he should intend] that the attributes of wisdom and understanding which are in his divine soul may be nullified and absorbed into the attributes of wisdom and understanding of the blessed *En Sof*, which are clothed, in particular, in the chapters of קדש and והיה כי יביאך.[8] That is to say, that he should use his wisdom and understanding that are in his soul, only for G-d alone. Similarly that the attribute of *da'at* that is in his soul, which includes both *chesed* (kindness) and *gevurah* (sternness), i.e., fear and love, in his heart, be nullified and absorbed into the attribute of the Higher Knowledge, which contains *chesed* and *gevurah* which is clothed in the chapters of שמע and והיה אם שמע.[9] This is what is written in the *Shulchan Aruch*:[10] "That he make his heart and brain subservient to Him," etc. And whilst putting on the *tzitzit* he should bear in mind, what is written in the *Zohar*, namely, to draw over himself His blessed Kingdom, which is the Kingdom over all worlds, etc., to bestow it particularly upon us through the commandment. And this corresponds to the subject of: "Thou shalt surely set a king over thee."[11]

In such a case, even though after all this [contemplation] no fear or dread descends upon him in a manifest manner in his heart, nevertheless since he accepts over himself the Kingdom of Heaven and draws fear of Him, blessed be He, over himself in his conscious thought and rational volition, and this submission is beyond doubt a sincere one—for it is the nature of all Jewish souls not to rebel against the blessed Holy King—then the Torah he studies or the commandment he performs because of this submission and because of this inspired fear in his mind, are termed "perfect service," like all service [performed] by a slave to his master or to his king.

On the other hand, if one studies and performs the commandment with love alone, in order to cleave to Him through

8. Two of the four parchment scrolls contained in the *tefillin* (phylacteries) are inscribed with the portions Exodus 13:1-10 and Exodus 13:11-16; the other two are mentioned below.
9. Deuteronomy 6:4-8 and Deuteronomy 11:13-21. See note above.
10. *Orach Chaim*, sec. 25, 5.
11. Deuteronomy 17:15.

His Torah or commandments, it is not termed "service of a servant," which is what the Torah demands, viz., "And ye shall serve the L-rd your G-d,"[12] etc., and "Him shall ye serve,"[13] etc., as explained in the *Zohar* (*Parshat Behar*): "Just like the ox on which one first places a yoke in order to make it useful to the world...so also must a human being first of all submit to the yoke of the Kingdom of Heaven...and if this submission is not found in him, holiness cannot rest on him,"[14] etc. (See also *Ra'aya Mehemna*, ibid., 111b) that every man must be of two categories and levels, namely, the category of a servant and that of a son. And although there is a son who is also a servant, it is not possible to attain to this degree without the prerequisite of *yirah ila'ah*, as is known to the initiated....

Without any fear at all, however, it does not soar on high through love alone, just as a bird cannot fly with one wing, for fear and love are the two wings (as has been explained in the *Tikkunim*). Similarly, fear alone is but one wing, and one's service cannot ascend on high with it, although it is termed the "service of a servant," for there must also be the filial quality, in order to awaken, at least, the natural love that is hidden in his heart, to become conscious of it in his mind at any rate, to be aware of his love of the One G-d in his thought and desire to cleave to Him, may He be blessed. This should be his *kavanah* when occupying himself with the Torah or the particular commandment, that his divine soul as well as his vivifying soul, together with their "garments," shall cleave to Him, as has been explained above.[15]

Yet in fact the Rabbis, of blessed memory, have said that a man should never separate himself from the community. Therefore he should intend to unite and attach to Him, blessed be He, the fount of his divine soul and the fount of the souls of all Israel, being the spirit of His blessed mouth, called by the name *Shechinah*, because it dwells and clothes itself in all worlds, animating them and giving them existence, and is that which imbues him with the power of speech to utter the words of Torah,

12. Exodus 23:25.
13. Deuteronomy 13:5.
14. *Zohar* III, p. 108a, with slight changes.
15. Chs. 23, 35, 37. See also ch. 14.

or with the power of action to perform the particular command-ment.

This union is attained through the drawing forth of the light of the blessed *En Sof* here below by means of occupation in the Torah and the commandments wherein [the light of the *En Sof*] is clothed....

Now, all his intent in the surrender of his soul to G-d through Torah and prayer, to elevate the spark of G-dliness therein back to its source, should be solely for the purpose of bringing gratifi-cation before Him, may He be blessed, as, for example, the joy of a king when his only son returns to him, being released from cap-tivity or imprisonment, as has been mentioned above.[16]

This *kavanah* is genuinely and truly sincere in every Jewish soul at every season and every hour, by virtue of the natural love which is a heritage bequeathed to us from our ancestors. Nevertheless one needs to establish set periods for reflecting on the greatness of G-d in order to attain intelligent fear and love, and with all that, perhaps one may succeed, as has been stated previously.

[*Tanya*, ch. 41, pp. 205-217.]

FEAR OF G-D

IN THE LIGHT OF WHAT HAS ALREADY been said on the subject of the lower kind of fear, one will clearly understand the Talmudic comment on the verse: "And now, O Israel, what doth the L-rd thy G-d require of thee, but to fear the L-rd thy G-d."[1] [The Gemara asks:] "Is fear, then, such a small thing?" [And the Gemara replies:] "Yes, in the case of Moses it was a small thing," and so forth.[2]

At first glance the answer is incomprehensible, for it is writ-ten: "What doth the L-rd require of *thee*?" [not of Moses]. The explanation, however, is as follows: Each and every soul of the

16. Ch. 31.

1. Deuteronomy 10:12.
2. *Brachot* 33b.

House of Israel contains within it something of the quality of our teacher Moses, peace unto him, for he is one of the "seven shepherds"[3] who cause vitality and G-dliness to flow to the community of the Jewish souls of Israel, for which reason they are called "shepherds." Our teacher, Moses, peace unto him, is the sum of them all, and he is called "the faithful shepherd." This means that he brings down the quality of da'at (knowledge) to the community of Israel that they may know the L-rd, each according to the capacity of his soul and its root above, and its nurture from the root of the soul of our teacher Moses, peace unto him, which is rooted in the Da'at Elyon (Higher Knowledge) of the ten sefirot of Atzilut, which are united with their blessed Emanator, for He and His Knowledge are One, and He is the Knowledge, etc.[4]

In addition and beyond this [general influence to the community as a whole] there descend, in every generation, sparks from the soul of our teacher Moses, peace unto him, and they clothe themselves in the body and soul of the sages of that generation, the "eyes" of the congregation,[5] to impart knowledge to the people that they may know the greatness of G-d and serve Him with heart and soul. For the service of the heart is according to the da'at (knowledge) as is written: "Know thou the G-d of thy father, and serve Him with a perfect heart and with a willing mind."[6]...

However, the essence of knowledge is not the knowing alone, that people should know the greatness of G-d from authors and books; but the essential thing is to immerse one's mind deeply into the greatness of G-d and fix one's thought on G-d with all the strength and vigor of the heart and mind, until his thought shall be bound to G-d with a strong and mighty bond, as it is bound to a material thing that he sees with his physical eyes and concentrates his thought on it.... This capacity and this quality of attaching one's "knowledge" to G-d is present in every soul of the House of Israel by virtue of its nurture from the soul of our teacher Moses, peace unto him. Only, since the soul has clothed

---

3. Sukkah 52b; another version in Tikkunim, end; Zohar Chadash (104a).
4. Ref. to Maimonides' statement already quoted in chs. 2, 4, 23.
5. See Taanit 24a and Rashi, loc. cit.; Numbers 16:24.
6. I Chronicles 28:9.

itself in the body, it needs a great and mighty exertion....

Now, therefore, each individual Jew, whoever he may be, when he ponders upon this for some considerable time each day—how the Holy One, blessed be He, is truly omnipresent in the higher and lower [worlds], and in reality fills the heavens and the earth, and that the whole world is truly full of His glory, and that He looks and regards and searches his reins and his heart and all his actions and words, and counts his every step—then fear will be implanted in his heart throughout the day; and when he again meditates on this, even with a superficial reflection, at any time or moment, he will turn away from evil and do good, in thought, speech and deed, so as not to rebel, G-d forbid, in the sight of His glory whereof the whole world is full....

This, then, is what the verse means: "But to fear the L-rd thy G-d, to walk in all His ways."[7] For this is the fear that leads to the fulfillment of His blessed commandments through turning away from evil and doing good. This is the "lower fear" which has been discussed earlier. As it applies to "Moses," that is to say, in relation to the quality of *da'at* that is in each divine Jewish soul, this is a minor thing, as has been stated above. (For *da'at* is [the faculty] which binds the hidden understanding of the heart with that which is actually revealed in thought, as is known to those who are familiar with the Esoteric Discipline)....

[*Tanya*, ch. 42, pp. 217-227.]

...AND LOVE OF G-D

CONCERNING THIS *YIRAH TATA'AH* ("lower fear"), which is directed toward the fulfillment of His commandments, in both areas of "depart from evil and do good," it was said, "Where there is no fear [of G-d], there is no wisdom."[1] It comprises a quality of "smallness"[2] and a quality of "greatness. The later being the quality of fear that has its origin in contemplation on the greatness of G-d....

---

7. Deuteronomy 10:12.

1. *Avot* 3:17.
2. Referring to the "natural" fear defined in chs. 41 and 42.

As for the *yirah ila'ah* ("higher fear"), however, a fear stemming from a sense of shame, an inner fear that derives from the inward aspects of G-dliness within the worlds, it was said concerning it that "where there is no wisdom, there is no fear."[3]...

However, one cannot attain to this fear and wisdom except in the fulfillment of the Torah and commandments through the lower, external fear. And this is what is meant by the statement: "Where there is no fear, there is no wisdom."[4]

Now, in love, too, there are two grades—*ahava rabbah* ("great love") and *ahavat olam* ("eternal love").[5] "Great love" is an ecstatic love, and it is "a fiery flame that rises of itself." It comes from above in a manner of a "gift" to him who is perfect in fear....

Ahavat olam, however, is that which comes from the understanding and knowledge of the greatness of G-d, the blessed *En Sof*, Who fills all worlds and encompasses all worlds and before Whom everything is accounted as nothing at all, like the nullity of one utterance within the intelligent soul while it still remains in its thought or in the desire of the heart, as has been explained earlier.[6] For as a result of such contemplation the attribute of love that is in the soul, will be divested of its garments, i.e., it will not clothe itself in anything of pleasure or enjoyment, whether physical or spiritual, to love it, and will not desire anything whatever in the world other than G-d alone, the Source of the vitality of all enjoyments, for they are all nullified in reality and are accounted as nothing at all, compared with Him, there being no manner of comparison or similitude between them, G-d forbid, just as there is no comparison between that which is absolutely nought and nothing—and everlasting life. As is written: "Whom have I in heaven [but Thee]? And there is nothing upon earth that I desire with Thee. My flesh and my heart yearn, O Rock of my heart,"[7] etc. And as will be explained later.[8]...

[*Tanya*, ch. 43, pp. 227-229.]

---

3. *Avot* 3:17.
4. Ibid.
5. Lit. "worldly" love, i.e. of this world, a love of G-d derived from contemplation of G-d in nature, as explained later on.
6. Ch. 20.
7. Psalms 73:25-26.
8. Ch. 48.

DIMENSIONS OF LOVE

EACH OF THE SAID TWO GRADES of love—the "great love" and the "eternal love"—is subdivided into many shades and gradations without limit, in each individual according to his capacity....

Yet there is one love which incorporates something of all the distinctions and gradations of both "great love" and "eternal love," and equally belongs in every Jewish soul, as our inheritance from our Patriarchs. And that is what the *Zohar* says on the verse: "[Thou art] my soul; I desire Thee in the night,"[1] etc., that "one should love the Holy One, blessed be He, with a love of the soul and the spirit, as these are attached to the body, and the body loves them," and so forth.[2] This is the interpretation of the verse: "My soul, I desire Thee," which means "Since Thou, O L-rd, art my true soul and life, therefore do I desire Thee." That is to say, "I long and yearn for Thee like a man who craves the life of his soul, and when he is weak and exhausted he longs and yearns for his soul to revive in him; and also when he goes to sleep he longs and yearns for his soul to be restored to him when he awakens from his sleep. So do I long and yearn to draw the light of the blessed *En Sof*, the Life of true life, within me through occupation in the Torah...." A great and more intense love than that— one which is likewise concealed in every soul of Israel as an inheritance from our ancestors—is that which is defined in *Ra'aya Mehemna* "Like a son who strives for the sake of his father and mother, whom he loves even more than his own body, soul, and spirit," etc.,[3] for "have we not all one Father?"[4]

And although [one may ask], Who is the man and where is he, who dares presume in his heart to approach and attain even a thousandth part of the degree of love of "the faithful shepherd" [Moses]? Nevertheless a minute portion and particle of his great

---

1. Isaiah 26:9.
2. *Zohar* III, 67a. This love of G-d is equated with the love of life itself—some-what less altruistic than the love defined further on.
3. Cf. end ch. 10 and ch. 43.
4. Malachi 2:10.

goodness and light illumines the community of Israel in each generation, as is stated in the *Tikkunim*[5] that "an emanation from him is present in every generation" "to illumine them,"[6] and so forth. Only, this glow is in a manner of great occultation and concealment in the souls of all Israel. But to bring forth this hidden love from its delitescence and concealment to [a state of] revelation, to be manifest in his heart and mind, this is "not beyond reach nor is it afar off, but the word is very nigh unto thee, in thy mouth and in thy heart."[7] That is to say, it should be habitual on his tongue and voice to arouse the intention of his heart and mind, so as to immerse his thought in the Life of life, the blessed *En Sof*, for He is literally our true Father and the Source of our life, and to awaken our love for Him like the love of a son for his father. And when he accustoms himself to this continually, habit will become nature.

Even if it appears to him at first sight that this is an illusion, he need not be concerned, because it is intrinsically the absolute truth by virtue of the "hidden love." But the purpose of its emergence into the open is in order to translate it into action, namely, the occupation in the Torah and commandments which he studies and performs as a result of it, with the intention to bring gratification before Him, may He be blessed, like a son serving his father....

[*Tanya*, ch. 44, pp. 231-235.]

COMPASSION

THERE IS YET ANOTHER DIRECT ROAD open to man, namely, to occupy himself with the Torah and commandments for their own sake through the attribute of our Patriarch Jacob, peace unto him, this being the attribute of mercy. It is first to arouse in his mind great compassion before G-d for the Divine spark which animates his soul that has descended from its Source, the Life of life, the blessed *En Sof*, Who pervades all worlds and transcends

---

5. *Tikkun* 69, pp. 112a, 114a. Cf. *Iggeret Hakodesh*, end ch. 27.
6. Cf. *Zohar* III, 216b, 273a.
7. Deuteronomy 30:11-12.

all worlds and in comparison with Whom everything is account-ed as nothing. Yet it [this spark] has been clothed in a "serpent's skin" which is far removed from the light of the King's counte-nance, at the greatest possible distance, since this world is the nadir of the coarse *kelipot*, etc....

In this way, a person is able to attain the distinction of *ahava rabbah* ("great love") in the consciousness of his heart, as is writ-ten: "Of Jacob, who redeemed Abraham," as has been explained elsewhere.

[*Tanya*, ch. 45, pp. 237-239.]

THERE IS YET ANOTHER GOOD WAY FOR A MAN, which is suitable for all and "very nigh" indeed, to arouse and kindle the light of the love that is implanted and concealed in his heart, that it may shine forth with its intense light, like a burning fire, in the con-sciousness of the heart and mind, to surrender his soul to G-d, together with his body and [material] possessions, with all his heart, and all his soul and all his might, from the depth of the heart, in absolute truth, especially at the time of the recital of the *Shema* and its blessings, as will be explained.

This [way] is: to take to heart the meaning of the verse: "As in water, face answereth to face, so does the heart of man to man."[1] This means that as [in the case of] the likeness and features of the face which a man presents to the water, the same identical face is reflected back to him from the water, so indeed is also the heart of a man who is loyal in his affection for another person, for this love awakens a loving response for him in the heart of his friend also, cementing their mutual love and loyalty for each other, especially as each sees his friend's love for him. Such is the com-mon nature in the character of every man even when they are equal in status. How much more so when a great and mighty king shows his great and intense love for a commoner who is despised and lowly among men, a disgraceful creature cast on the dunghill, yet he [the king] comes down to him from the place of his glory, together with all his retinue, and raises him and exalts him from his dunghill and brings him into his palace, the royal palace, in the innermost chamber, a place such as no servant or lord ever

---

1. Proverbs 27:19.

enters, and there shares with him the closest companionship with embraces and kisses and spiritual attachment[2] with all heart and soul—how much more will, of itself, be aroused a doubled and redoubled love in the heart of this most common and humble individual for the person of the king, with a true attachment of spirit, heart and soul, and with infinite heartfelt sincerity. Even if his heart be like a heart of stone, it will surely melt and become water, and his soul will pour itself out like water, with soulful longing for the love of the king.

In a manner corresponding in every detail to the said figure and image, but to an infinitely greater degree, has the L-rd our G-d dealt with us. For His greatness is beyond comprehension, and He pervades all worlds and transcends all worlds; and from the holy Zohar, as also from our Master Rabbi Isaac Luria of blessed memory, it is known of the infinite multitude of *hechalot* and worlds, and of the countless myriads of angels in each world and *hechal*....

All these [angels] ask: "Where is the place of His glory?" And they answer: "The whole earth is full of His glory,"[3] that is, His people, Israel. For the Holy One, blessed be He, forsakes the higher and lower creatures choosing none of them but Israel His people, whom He brought out of Egypt...in order to bring them near to Him in true closeness and unity, with a truly soulful attachment on the level of "kisses" of mouth to mouth, by means of uttering the word of G-d, namely, the Halachah, and the fusion of spirit to spirit, namely, the comprehension of the Torah and the knowledge of His will and wisdom, all of which is truly one [with G-d]; also with a form of "embrace," namely, the fulfillment of the positive precepts with the 248 organs, for the 248 ordinances are the 248 "organs" of the King, as has been explained.[4]...

This is the meaning of [the text of the benedictions] "Who hath sanctified us by His commandments": like one who

---

2. "Embraces"—performance of the precepts; "kisses"—precepts performed orally (esp. prayer); "spiritual attachment" (lit. "attachment of spirit to spirit")—meditation and comprehension. In other words, complete communion by thought, word, and deed.

3. Isaiah 6:3.

4. Ch. 23.

betrothes[5] a wife that she may be united with him with a perfect bond, as is written: "And he shall cleave to his wife, and they shall be one flesh."[6] Exactly similar, and even infinitely surpassing, is the union of the divine soul that is occupied in Torah and commandments, and of the vivifying soul, and their garments referred to above, with the light of the blessed *En Sof*....

[*Tanya*, ch. 46, pp. 241-245.]

EXODUS: PERSONAL EXPERIENCE

"IN EVERY GENERATION AND EVERY DAY a person is obliged to regard himself as if he has that day come out of Egypt."[1] This refers to the release of the divine soul from the confinement of the body, the "serpent's skin," in order to be absorbed into the Unity of the light of the blessed *En Sof*, through occupation in the Torah and commandments in general, and in particular through accepting the Kingdom of Heaven during the recital of the *Shema*, wherein the person explicitly accepts and draws over himself His blessed Unity, when he says: "The Lord is our G-d, the Lord is One."[2]... The only thing that precludes us from the attachment of the soul to His Blessed Unity and light is the will, that is, if the human being does not will it at all, G-d forbid, to cleave to Him, etc. But immediately he does so desire, and he accepts and draws upon himself His blessed G-dliness and declares: "The L-rd is our G-d, the L-rd is One," then surely is his soul spontaneously absorbed into His blessed Unity, for "spirit evokes spirit, and draws forth spirit."[3] This is a form of "Exodus from Egypt." Therefore it was ordained that the paragraph concerning the Exodus from Egypt be read specifically during the

---

5. The word קדשנו ("who sanctified us") may be rendered "who has betrothed us" (קידושין—betrothal).
6. Genesis 2:24

1. The Mishnah (*Pesachim* 10:5) does not contain the words "and every day" and "that day," which the author inserts.
2. Deuteronomy 6:4.
3. I.e. bestows an extra measure of spirituality. *Zohar* II, 162b.

recital of the *Shema*,[4] although it is a commandment by itself, and not appertaining to the commandment of the recital of the *Shema*, as is stated in the Talmud and Codes,[5] for they are actually the same thing....

[*Tanya*. ch. 47, pp. 247-249.]

G-D'S IMMANENCE AND TRANSCENDENCE

CONTEMPLATING ON THE GREATNESS of the blessed *En Sof*, the intelligent person [will realize] that as His name indicates, so is He—there is no end, or limit, or finitude at all to the light and vitality that diffuse from Him, may He be blessed, by His simple[1] will, and which is united with His blessed essence and being in perfect unity. Had the worlds descended from the light of the blessed *En Sof* without "contractions,"[2] but according to a gradual descent, from grade to grade by means of cause and effect—this world would not, in such case, have ever been created in its present form, in a finite and limited order.... Even the World to Come and the Supreme Garden of Eden—the habitation of the souls of the great *tzaddikim*—and the souls themselves and, needless to add, the angels—are all in the realm of bounds and limitation, for there is a limit to their apprehension of the light of the blessed *En Sof*, which shines on them through being clothed in ChaBaD, etc., hence, there is also a boundary to their enjoyment derived from the splendor of the *Shechinah*, and to their pleasure in the light of G-d; for they cannot absorb enjoyment and delight of an infinite order, without being nullified out of their existence and returned to their source.

Now, as for the intricate details of the "contractions"—this is

---

4. Cf. *Brachot* 13a; Rabbi Schneur Zalman of Liadi, *Shulchan Aruch, Orach Chaim* 58:1.
5. *Brachot* 21a; ibid., 67:1-2.

1. I.e. uncaused.
2. The doctrine of *tzimtzum* has already been referred to previously in chs. 21 and 38. Here and in the next chapter, it is further expanded.

not the place for their explanation.[3] But in general they are something in the nature of "occupation and concealment" of the flow of the light and vitality, so that only an extremely minute portion of light and vitality should illuminate and reach the lower creatures in a revealed manner, as it were, pervading them and acting in them and animating them so that they might receive existence *ex nihilo*, and be in a state of finitude and limitation. This constitutes an exceedingly contracted illumination, and it is considered as virtually nothing at all compared with the quality of the limitless and infinite illumination, and there is no reference or relationship between them, as the term "reference" is understood in values, where the figure 1 has a relevancy with the number 1,000,000, for it is one millionth part of it; but as regards a thing which is in the realm of infinity, there is no number that can be considered relative to it, for a billion or trillion do not attain the relevancy of the figure 1 in comparison with a billion or trillion, but is veritably accounted as nothing.

So, indeed, is the quality of the contracted illumination which informs the higher and lower worlds, acting in them and animating them—compared with the quality of the hidden and concealed light that is of an infinite order and does not clothe itself or exercise its influence in the worlds, to animate them in a revealed manner, but it "encompasses" them from above and is called *sovev kol almin* (the "Encompasser of all Worlds"). The meaning of this is not that it encircles and encompasses from above spatially, G-d forbid, for in spiritual matters the category of space is in no way applicable. But the meaning is that it "encircles and encompasses from above" insofar as the so-called "revealed" influence is concerned, for influence which is in the category of "revelation" in the worlds, is referred to as "investiture," being "clothed" within the worlds, for the influence that they receive is clothed and comprehended by them; whereas the influence which does not come within the category of "revelation," but remains in occultation and concealment and is not apprehended by the worlds, is not described as being "invested" but as "encircling and encompassing." Therefore, since the

---

3. See *Torah Or*, p. 27a; *Likkutei Torah, Vayikra* p. 101 ff.; *Ekev* p. 33 ff. See also Translator's Introduction to *Likkutei Amarim*, Part II.

worlds belong in the order of the finite and limited, it follows that only an extremely minute and contracted reflection of the flow of the light of the blessed *En Sof* clothes and reveals itself in them in a revealed form, and this, only to animate them in a finite and limited state. But the principal light without contraction to such an extent, is called *makif* ("encircler") and *sovev* ("encompasser"), since its influence is not revealed within them, inasmuch as they belong in the order of the finite and the limited.

To illustrate this point, consider this material world. Even though "the whole world is full of His glory,"[4] namely, the light of the blessed *En Sof*, as is written: "Do not I fill heaven and earth? saith the L-rd,"[5] nevertheless only a very small vitality, of the category of inanimate and vegetable worlds, is clothed therein in the form of "revealed" influence, while all the light of the blessed *En Sof* is termed as "encompassing" it, even though it actually pervades it, since its influence is no more revealed in it, but is active in it in a hidden and concealed manner; and any influence of a concealed nature is referred to as "encircling from above," for the "hidden world" is on a higher plane than the "revealed world."

Let us make it more intelligible by means of an example. When a man forms an image in his mind of something that he has seen or sees—although the entire body and essence of that thing, both its exterior and interior and its very core, are completely mirrored in his mind and thought, for he has seen it or is seeing it in its entirety—this is expressed by saying that his mind encompasses that object completely, and that thing is enveloped by his mind and thought. But it is not encompassed in actual fact, only in the imagination of the man's thought and mind.

The Holy One, blessed be He, however, of Whom it is written: "For My thoughts are not your thoughts,"[6] etc., surely His Thought and Mind knowing all created things, encompass each and every created being from its beginning to its end and its inside and very core, all in actual reality.

For example, in the case of the orb of this earth, His blessed knowledge encompasses the entire diameter of the globe of the

4. Isaiah 6:3.
5. Jeremiah 23:24.
6. Isaiah 55:8.

Earth, together with all that is in it and its deepest interior to its lowest depths, all in actual reality. For this knowledge constitutes the vitality of the whole spherical thickness of the Earth and its creations *ex nihilo*. However, it would not have come into being as it now is, as a finite and limited thing, with an exceedingly minute vitality sufficient for the categories of inorganic matter and vegetation, were it not for the many powerful contractions which have condensed the light and vitality that is clothed in the orb of the earth, so as to animate it and sustain it in its finite and limited status and in the categories of inorganic and vegetable matter alone.

But His blessed knowledge which is united with His essence and being—for "He is the Knowledge, the Knower, and the Known, and knowing Himself, as it were, He knows all created things, but not with a knowledge that is external to Himself, like the knowledge of a human being, for all of them [the created things] are derived from His blessed Reality, and this thing is not within the power of human beings to comprehend clearly," and so forth[7]—this knowledge, since it is of an infinite order, is not described as clothing itself in the orb of the earth, which is finite and limited, but as encircling and encompassing it, although this knowledge embraces its entire thickness and interior in actual reality, giving it existence *ex nihilo*, as is explained elsewhere.

[*Tanya*, ch. 48, pp. 240-255.]

ADVANCE AND RETREAT

EVEN THOUGH THE PARTICULAR ASPECTS of the nature of the occultation and concealment of the light of the blessed *En Sof* in the descent of the worlds—until this material world was created—are too numerous to count and are of many diverse kinds, as is known to those who have tasted of the Tree of Life,[1] yet in general there are three levels of powerful and comprehensive "contractions," giving rise to three comprehensive worlds, each category consisting of myriads upon myriads of particulars. These are

---

7. Maimonides, *Code*, *Hilchot Yesodei Hatorah*, 2:10; cf. *Tanya*, beg. ch. 2.

1. The Kabbalah.

the three worlds of *Beriah, Yetzirah* and *Asiyah*, for the world of *Atzilut* is G-dliness itself.

In order to create the world of *Beriah*, which consists of the higher souls and angels, whose service to G-d is in the sphere of ChaBaD [the intellectual faculties] which are clothed in them and are apprehended by them and from which they receive influence, there preceded a powerful "contraction," as mentioned above.

So, too, from *Beriah* to *Yetzirah*. For the minute portion of light which clothes itself in the world of *Beriah* is still in a category of infinity in relation to the world of *Yetzirah*, and is unable to clothe itself in the latter except through a contraction and occultation. So, too, from *Yetzirah* to *Asiyah*.

(An elaborate explanation of these three "contractions," in order to make them more accessible to our poor intellect is given elsewhere.[2])

The purpose of all the "contractions" is the creation of the material human body and the subjugation of the *sitra achra*, to bring about the preeminence of light supplanting darkness—when a person elevates his divine soul and his vivifying soul together with their garments and all the powers of the body, to G-d alone, as has been discussed earlier at length,[3] for this is the purpose of the descent of the worlds.

To quote [again] "as water mirrors the reflection of a face": As the Holy One, blessed be He, has, as it were, laid down and set aside, figuratively speaking, His great Infinite Light, and has stored it away and concealed it by means of three different kinds of "contractions"—and all this because of His love for lowly man, in order to raise him up to G-d, for "love impels the flesh,"[4] how much more, and an infinite number of times more, is it fitting that a man also should relinquish and set aside all he possesses, both spiritually and physically, and renounce everything in order to cleave to Him, may He be blessed, with attachment, desire and longing, without any hindrance, within or without, neither of

---

2. The doctrine of *tzimtzum* is more fully discussed in the second part of the *Tanya* (*Shaar Hayichud v'haEmunah*).

3. Chs. 35-37.

4. *Bava Metzia* 84a.

body nor soul, nor money, nor wife and children....

[*Tanya*, ch. 49, pp. 255-257.]

THERE IS, HOWEVER, YET ANOTHER distinction of love which excels them all, as gold is superior to silver, and this is a love like fiery coals from the distinction of the "Supernal *Gevurot*" from *Binah ila'ah* ("Supernal Understanding").[1] This is when, through contemplation on the greatness of the blessed *En Sof*, before whom everything is truly accounted as nought, the soul is kindled and flares up towards the glory of the splendor of His greatness, in order to gaze on the glory of the King, like glowing coals of a mighty flame which surges upwards, striving to be parted from the wick and the wood on which it has taken hold. This is brought on by the preponderance of the element of Divine fire that is in the divine soul. In consequence of this it develops a thirst, as is written: "My soul thirsteth for Thee";[2] next it attains the distinction of "love-sickness";[3] and then it reaches a state of very rapture of the soul (כלות הנפש) as is written: "Yea, my soul is enraptured."[4]...

The order of the service in occupying oneself with the Torah and commandments, a service derived from the category of the said intense love, is in the manner of "retreat" alone, as is written in *Sefer Yetzirah*: "And if thy heart hastens, return to the One."[5] The interpretation of [the phrase] "if thy heart hastens" is the craving of the soul that is in the right side of the heart—when it gains sway[6] and bursts into flame and grows so exceedingly enraptured that the very soul is consumed with a desire to pour itself out into the embrace of its Father, the blessed Life of life, and to leave its confinement in the corporeal, physical body, in order to attach itself to Him, may He be blessed—then one must take to heart the teaching of the Rabbis, of blessed memory: "Despite

---

1. *Chochmah* and *Binah* in the intellect have their counterparts *chesed* and *gevurah* in the *middot*.
2. Psalms 63:2.
3. Song of Songs 2:5.
4. Psalms 84:3.
5. 1:8. Cf. Introduction to *Tikkunei Zohar* 7a.
6. ...over the left pact, i.e. over the natural desires of the animal soul.

thyself thou livest"[7] in this body, animating it for the purpose of drawing downwards the higher life from the blessed Life of life, through the life-giving Torah, that there may be a dwelling in the lower world for His blessed Oneness in a revealed state. As has been explained above, and as is explained in the holy *Zohar*,[8] "that there be 'One in One,' the meaning of which is that the *yichud hane'elam* (hidden Unity) shall become a category of the "revealed world.".…

[*Tanya.* ch. 50, pp. 263-265.]

SHECHINAH

TO RETURN TO, AND FURTHER TO ELUCIDATE, the expression of the *Yenuka*, mentioned earlier,[1] it is necessary first to explain—so that one may understand a little—the subject of the indwelling of the *Shechinah*, which rested in the Holy of Holies and likewise, all other places where the *Shechinah* rested. —What is the meaning of this? Is not the whole world full of His glory? And surely there is no place void of Him.

The [clue to the] understanding of this is to be found in the text: "From my flesh I see G-d."[2] The analogy is from the soul of a human being which pervades all the 248 organs of the body, from head to foot, yet its principal habitation and abode is in his brain, whence it is diffused throughout all the organs, each of which receives from it vitality and power appropriate to it, according to its composition and character: the eye for seeing, the ear for hearing, the mouth for speaking, and the feet for walking—as we clearly sense it that in the brain one is conscious of everything that is affected in the 248 organs and everything that is experienced by them.

Now, the variation in the acquisition of power and vitality by the organs of the body from the soul, is not due to the [soul's]

---

7. *Avot* 4:22.
8. II, 135a.

1. Ch. 35.
2. Job 19:26.

essence and being, for this would make its quiddity and essence divisible into 248 diverse parts, vested in 248 *loci* according to the various forms and locations of the organs of the body. If this were so, it would follow that its essence and quiddity are fashioned in a material design, in a likeness and form resembling the shape of the body, Heaven forfend! Rather, it is entirely a single and simple spiritual entity, which, by its intrinsic essence, is divested of any corporeal shape and of any category and dimension of space, size, or physical limitation. It is, therefore, impertinent to say, in relation to its quiddity and essence, that it is located in the brain of the head more than it is in the feet, since its quiddity and essence are not subject to the dimensions and categories of physical limitation. But there are contained in it, in its intrinsic essence, 613 kinds of powers and vitalities to be actualized and to emerge from concealment in order to animate the 248 organs and 365 veins of the body, through their embodiment in the vivifying soul, which also possesses the corresponding 248 and 365 powers and vitalities.

It is with reference to the flow of all the 613 kinds of powers and vitalities from the concealment of the soul into the body in the process of animating it, that it has been said that the principal dwelling place and abode of this flow of life and of this manifestation is situated entirely in the brains of the head. Therefore they first receive the power and vitality appropriate to them according to their disposition and character, namely, ChaBaD (*chochmah, binah, da'at*) and the faculty of thought, and all that pertains to the brains; and not only this, but also the sum-total of all the streams of vitality flowing to the other organs is also contained and is clothed in the brain that is in the head. It is there that the core and root of the said manifest flow of the light and vitality of the whole soul are to be found. From there a radiation is diffused to all the other organs, each of which receives the power and vitality appropriate to it in accordance with its disposition and character: the faculty of sight reveals itself in the eye, and the faculty of hearing manifests itself in the ear, and so forth. But all the powers flow from the brain, as is known, for therein is located the principal dwelling-place of the whole soul, in its manifest aspect, since the sum-total of the vitality that is diffused from it is revealed there. Only, the [individual] powers of the said general vitality shine forth and are radiated from there into all the organs of the body, much in the same manner as light radiates from the sun and penetrates rooms within rooms. (Even the heart receives vitality from the brain; hence the brain has an intrinsic supremacy over it, as has been explained above.)[3]

In a truly like manner, figuratively speaking, does the blessed En Sof fill all worlds and animate them. And in each world there are creatures without limit or end, myriads upon myriads of various grades of angels and souls, etc., and so, too, is the abundance of the worlds without end or limit, one higher than the other, etc.

Now, the quiddity and essence of the blessed En Sof is the same in the higher and lower worlds, as in the example with the soul given above, and as is written in the Tikkunim that "He is the Hidden One of all the hidden."[4] This is to be understood that even in the higher, hidden worlds He is hidden and concealed within them, just as He is hidden and concealed in the lower, for no thought can apprehend Him at all even in the higher worlds. Thus as He is to be found there, so is He found in the very lowest.

The difference between the higher and lower worlds is with regard to the stream of vitality which the blessed En Sof causes to flow and illumine in a category of "revealment out of concealment" (which is one of the reasons why the influence and stream of this vitality is figuratively called "light"), thereby animating the worlds and the creatures therein. For the higher worlds receive in a somewhat more "revealed" form than do the lower; and all creatures therein receive each according to its capacity and nature, which is the nature and the form of the particular flow with which the blessed En Sof imbues and illumines it.

But the lower [worlds], even the spiritual ones, do not receive [the light] in quite such a "revealed" form, but only by means of many "garments," wherein the blessed En Sof invests the vitality and light which He causes to flow and shine on them in order to animate them. These garments, wherein the blessed En Sof invests and conceals the light and vitality, are so numerous and powerful that thereby He created this very corporeal and physi-

---

3. Ch. 12.
4. *Tikkunei Zohar*, Intro. 17a.

cal world. He gives it existence and animates it by the vitality and light which He causes to flow and shine forth into it—a light that is clothed, hidden and concealed within the numerous and powerful garments, which hide and screen the light and vitality, so that no light or vitality whatever is visibly revealed, but only corporeal and physical things that appear lifeless. Yet they contain light and vitality that constantly give them existence *ex nihilo*, that they shall not revert and become nothing and nought as they had been....

[*Tanya*, ch. 51, pp. 265-271.]

SOURCE OF LIFE

NOW, JUST AS IN THE HUMAN SOUL the principal manifestation of the general vitality is in the brain, while all the organs receive merely a light and potency which shines on them from the source of the manifestation of the said vitality in the brain, so indeed, figuratively speaking, is the essential manifestation of the general stream of vitality, animating the worlds and the creatures therein, clothed and contained in His blessed will, wisdom, understanding and knowledge, which are called the "intelligence," and these are they that are clothed in the Torah and its commandments.

The manifestation of this general flow of life is the source of the vitality which the worlds receive, each one in particular. Only a glow is diffused and shines forth from this source in a similar manner as the light radiates from the sun, by way of example, or as the powers of the organs of the body derive from the brain, as discussed above.[1]

It is this source which is called the "world of manifestation" or "matron," or "nether matriarch," or "*Shechinah*,"[2] from the Scriptural phrase: "That I may dwell among them."[3] For this source is the beginning of the revelation of the light of *En Sof*, which extends to, and illumines, the worlds in a "revealed" manner. From this source there extends to each individual thing the

1. In the previous chapter.
2. Literally "indwelling," from the word ושכנתי in the quoted verse.
3. Exodus 25:8.

particular light and vitality suitable to it, and it [the light] dwells and is clothed in them, thereby animating them. Therefore it is figuratively called "mother of the children," and "community of Israel," for from this source have emanated the souls of *Atzilut* and have been created the souls of *Beriah*, and so forth, all of them being derived only from the extension of the vitality and light from this source which is called "*Shechinah*," resembling the radiation of light from the sun.

But as for the *Shechinah* itself, namely, the origin and core of the manifestation whereby the blessed *En Sof* illumines the worlds in a "revealed" form and which is the source of all the streams of vitality in all the worlds (their entire vitality being no more than the light that is diffused from it like the light radiated from the sun), the worlds cannot endure or receive the light of this *Shechinah*, that it might actually dwell and clothe itself in them—without a "garment" to screen and conceal its light from them, so that they may not become entirely nullified and lose their identity within their source, like the nullification of the light of the sun in its source, namely, in the sun itself, where this light cannot be seen, but only the integral mass of the sun itself.

But what is this "garment" which is able to conceal and clothe [the *Shechinah*] yet will not [itself] be completely nullified within its light? This is His blessed will and wisdom, and so forth, which are clothed in the Torah and its commandments that are revealed to us and to our children, for "the Torah issues from wisdom,"[4] which is *chochmah ila'ah* ("Supernal Wisdom") that is immeasurably higher than the world of manifestation, for "He is wise, but not with a knowable wisdom," and so forth. And as has previously been explained, the light of the blessed *En Sof* is clothed in and united with the Supernal Wisdom, and He, may He be blessed, and His wisdom are One, only that it has descended by means of obscuring gradations, from grade to grade, with the descent of the worlds, until it has clothed itself in material things, namely, the 613 commandments of the Torah....

[*Tanya.* ch. 52, pp. 271-273.]

---

4. *Zohar* II, 85a and 121a.

WICK AND OIL: CONSUMMATION

THE 613 COMMANDMENTS OF THE TORAH, together with the seven commandments of our Rabbis, combine to total the numerical equivalent of כתר ("crown") which is the blessed *Ratzon Elyon* ("Supernal Will"), which is clothed in His blessed Wisdom, and they are united with the light of the blessed *En Sof* in a perfect union. "The L-rd by wisdom hath founded the earth,"[1] which refers to the Oral Law that is derived from the Higher Wisdom, as is written in the *Zohar*, "The Father [*chochmah*] begat the daughter[2] [i.e., *malchut*, the Oral Law]."

And this is what the *Yenuka* meant when he said that "the Supernal light that is kindled on one's head, namely, the *Shechinah*, requires oil,"[3] that is, to be clothed in wisdom, which is called "oil from the holy anointing,"[4] as is explained in the *Zohar*, that "these are the good deeds," namely, the 613 commandments, which derive from His blessed wisdom. Thereby the light of the *Shechinah* can cling to the wick, i.e. the vivifying soul in the body, which is metaphorically called a "wick." For just as in the case of a material candle, the light shines by virtue of the annihilation and burning of the wick turning to fire, so does the light of the *Shechinah* rest on the divine soul as a result of the annihilation of the animal soul and its transformation "from darkness to light and from bitterness to sweetness" in the case of the righteous, or at least through the destruction of its garments, which are thought, speech and action, and their transformation from the darkness of the *kelipot* to the Divine light of the blessed *En Sof*, which is clothed and united in the thought, speech and action of the 613 commandments of the Torah, in the case of *benonim*....

[*Tanya*, ch. 53, pp. 279-281.]

---

1. Proverbs 3:19.
2. *Zohar* III, 248a, 256b.
3. Ibid., 187a. Cf. *Tanya*, chs. 35, 51.
4. Exodus 30:31.

INDEX

INDEX

הוצאת ספרים
קרני הוד תורה
קה
ליובאוויטש